Armies of the
Steppe Nomads, 376–1227

Gabriele Esposito is a military historian who works as a freelance author and researcher for some of the most important publishing houses in the military history sector. In particular, he is an expert specializing in uniformology: his interests and expertise range from the ancient civilizations to modern post-colonial conflicts. During recent years, he has conducted and published several researches on the military history of the Latin American countries, with special attention on the War of the Triple Alliance and the War of the Pacific. He is among the leading experts on the military history of the Italian Wars of Unification and the Spanish Carlist Wars. His books and essays are published on a regular basis by Osprey Publishing, Winged Hussar Publishing and Libreria Editrice Goriziana. He is also the author of numerous military history articles appearing in specialized magazines such as *Ancient Warfare Magazine*, *Medieval Warfare Magazine*, *The Armourer*, *History of War*, *Guerres et Histoire*, *Focus Storia* and *Focus Storia Wars*.

Armies of the Steppe Nomads, 376–1227

From the Coming of Attila's Huns to the
Death of Genghis, Great Khan of the Mongols

Gabriele Esposito

Pen & Sword
MILITARY

First published in Great Britain in 2024 by
Pen & Sword Military
An imprint of
Pen & Sword Books Limited
Yorkshire – Philadelphia

Copyright © Pen & Sword Books Limited 2024

ISBN 978 1 39903 777 8

The right of Gabriele Esposito to be identified as
Author of this Work has been asserted by him in accordance
with the Copyright, Designs and Patents Act 1988.

A CIP catalogue record for this book is
available from the British Library

Typeset by Mac Style
Printed and bound in India by Replika Press Pvt Ltd.

Pen & Sword Books Limited incorporates the imprints of After the Battle,
Atlas, Archaeology, Aviation, Discovery, Family History, Fiction, History,
Maritime, Military, Military Classics, Politics, Select, Transport, True Crime,
Air World, Frontline Publishing, Leo Cooper, Remember When, Seaforth
Publishing, The Praetorian Press, Wharncliffe Local History, Wharncliffe
Transport, Wharncliffe True Crime and White Owl.

For a complete list of Pen & Sword titles please contact:

PEN & SWORD BOOKS LIMITED
47 Church Street, Barnsley, South Yorkshire, S70 2AS, England
E-mail: enquiries@pen-and-sword.co.uk
Website: www.pen-and-sword.co.uk
or
PEN AND SWORD BOOKS
1950 Lawrence Road, Havertown, PA 19083, USA
E-mail: uspen-and-sword@casematepublishers.com
Website: www.penandswordbooks.com

MIX
Paper | Supporting
responsible forestry
FSC™ C016779

Contents

Acknowledgements

This book is dedicated to my magnificent parents, Maria Rosaria and Benedetto, for the immense love and fundamental support that they always give me. Without their precious advice over countless years, this book would not have been possible. A very special thanks goes to Philip Sidnell, the commissioning editor of my books for Pen & Sword: his love for history and his passion for publishing are the key factors behind the success of our publications. Many thanks also to the production manager of this title, Matt Jones, for his excellent work and great enthusiasm. A special mention is due to Tony Walton for the magnificent work he performs editing all my books. A very special mention goes to the brilliant re-enactment groups that collaborated with their photographs to the creation of this book: without the incredible work of research of their members, the final result of this publication would have not been the same. As a result, I want to express my deep gratitude to the following living history associations: Iloncsuk Szabadcsapat, Isenbrand Saga, Nyugati Gyepűk Pajzsa Haditorna Egyesület and Tolnai-Turán Hagyományőrző Sportegyesület from Hungary; Association for restoration and preservation of Bulgarian traditions – Avitohol, Equestrian Martial Arts School – Madara horseman, Bulgarian School of Ancient Military Arts – Greatness, Jordan Sivkov – Leather Works, Kalina Atanasova – https://badamba.info/, Boris Bedrosov and Jasmin Parvanov from Bulgaria; Asociatia C.S. Nokors from Romania; Jan Kudělka from the Czech Republic; Scythian State from Ukraine; Hrafn Vaeringi from the United Kingdom; The Skjaldborg from the USA; Amages Drachen from Germany; and Les Seigneurs d'Orient from France.

Introduction

The main aim of this book is to present a detailed overview of the history, organization and equipment of the military forces deployed by the nomadic peoples of the steppes during the period AD 376–1227, from the appearance of the Huns in Eastern Europe to the death of Genghis Khan. For reasons of space, our analysis will be focused on the most important nomadic peoples interacting with the Ancient and Medieval civilizations of Europe, and thus will not cover some of those living only in Asia. Each chapter will be devoted to a different nomadic people, in order to present – in almost chronological order – a complete history of all the Eurasian civilizations that played a prominent military role during Antiquity and the Middle Ages. The first chapter will describe the first two nomadic peoples living on the Pontic Steppe – the Scythians, who interacted with the Greek world, and the Sarmatians, who interacted with the Roman world. The second chapter will deal with the Huns of Attila, whose migration was one of the key factors behind the fall of the Roman Empire, while the third chapter will be devoted to the Avars, who established a large state in Eastern Europe that rivalled that of Charlemagne. The fourth chapter will cover the Magyars, who terrorized most of Europe with their incursions during the tenth century before creating the Kingdom of Hungary, and the fifth chapter will reconstruct the history of the Bulgars, who became the fiercest enemies of the Byzantine Empire in the Balkans but also created a flourishing state in the Volga region of Russia. The sixth chapter will deal with the Khazars and the Alans, who dominated vast portions of southern Russia and stopped Arab expansionism in the Caucasus. The seventh chapter will be devoted to the Turks, who were for a long time a major power of the Eurasian steppes before playing a crucial role in the Crusades. The eighth chapter will cover the Pechenegs and the Cumans-Kipchaks, who were great military powers of the Eurasian steppes during a chaotic historical period, and finally the ninth chapter will focus on the history of the Mongols from the unification of their tribes to the death of the great Genghis Khan. By describing the military organization, weapons and tactics of these nomadic peoples, we will see how they dominated the battlefields of the European world for almost 2,000 years thanks to their superior fighting abilities. We will also examine how they interacted with other civilizations and how the latter learned so much from the steppe peoples, especially from a military point of view. Indeed, without the existence of the warlike nomadic peoples of the Eurasian steppes, the history of Europe and even the whole world would have been completely different.

Chapter 1

The Early Nomadic Peoples

The first two nomadic peoples to emerge in the vast steppes of Eastern Europe were the Scythians and the Sarmatians, who were part of the Indo-Europeans and originated in the heart of Central Asia, from where they migrated towards the vast plains of southern Russia and Ukraine. Like all the steppe peoples of Antiquity and the Middle Ages, the Scythians and Sarmatians were described as 'masters of horses' by the sedentary peoples living around them. Being nomads who were constantly on the move, the Scythians and Sarmatians spent most of their lives on horse, which was a fundamental component of their civilizations. Life was extremely harsh for these nomadic peoples: they did not practice agriculture but had large amounts of cattle. To find the pastures needed to feed these cattle, they moved across the wild plains of the steppe by following the course of major rivers. All the Scythian and Sarmatian men were warriors, who travelled on horseback; their families followed them on carts, which were the mobile homes of the steppe peoples. The Scythian and Sarmatian societies were quite simple and egalitarian, since all the free men had the right to bear arms and to fight in case of war. There was a powerful nobility made up of warlords and their personal retainers, but these did not enjoy particular privileges. The individuals tasked with performing religious rites, made up a separate component of the Scythian and Sarmatian societies, these priests being the guardians of their people's traditions. Both the Scythians and Sarmatians owned slaves, who were foreigners captured during military incursions or individuals from the local communities of southern Russia and Ukraine who had been submitted by the steppe peoples during their migrations. Slave trading always remained an important economic activity of the Scythians and Sarmatians. However, it should be noted that these two steppe peoples were extremely advanced culturally. First of all, their women enjoyed a series of liberties that could not be found in any other society of the Ancient world: they were permitted to live and fight as men and enjoyed the same rights. Indeed, the famous myth of the Amazons originated after the Greeks met with the warrior women of the Scythians. The Scythians and Sarmatians were the first peoples in history, together with the Cimmerians and the Massagetae, to deploy massive cavalry armies. These military forces were totally different from those of their opponents from the Mediterranean world or Mesopotamia, which mostly

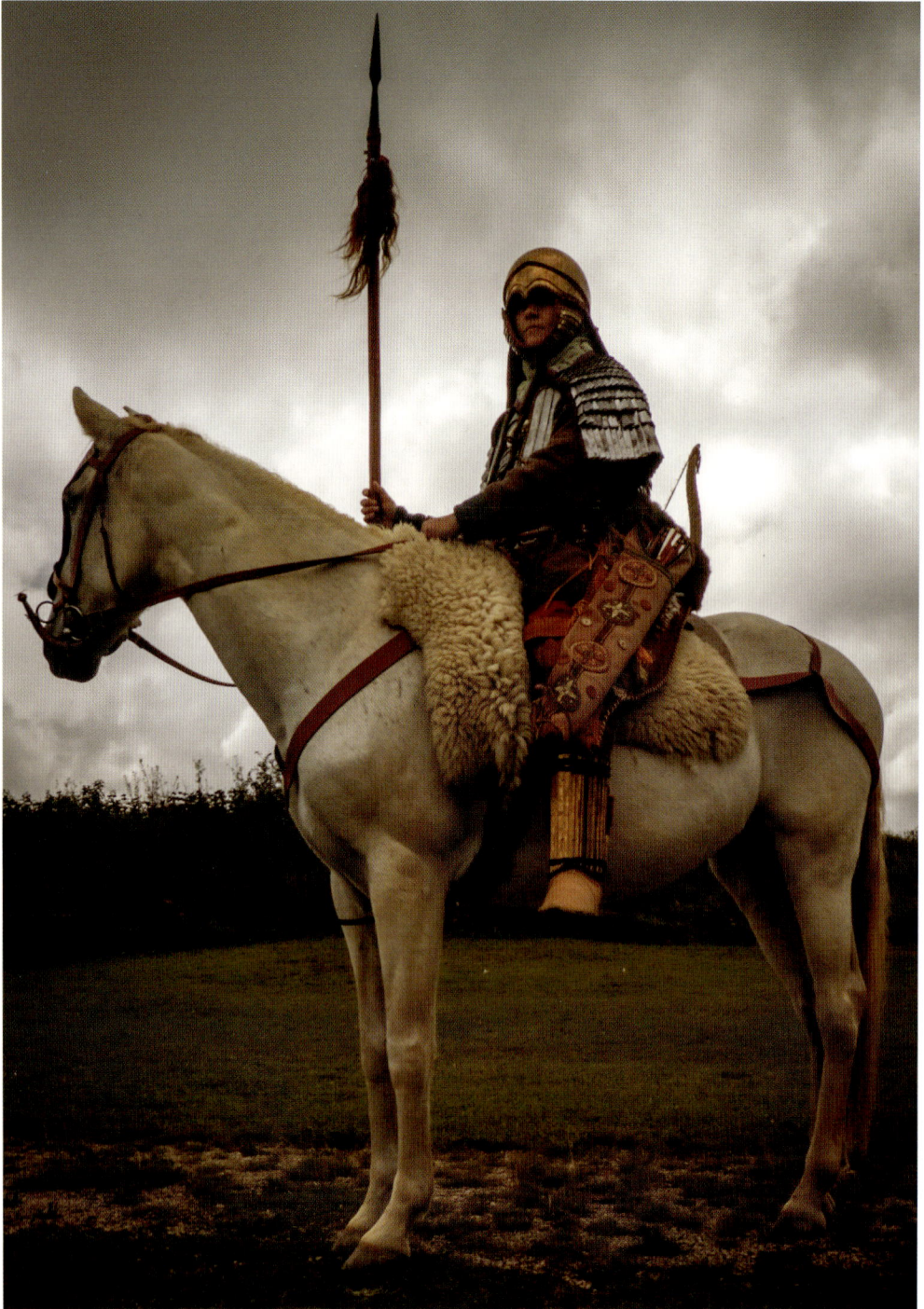

Scythian heavy cavalryman equipped with a spear and composite bow.
(*Photo and copyright by Amages Drachen*)

consisted of infantry. Riding sturdy horses and equipped with deadly composite bows, the Scythian mounted archers faced – and on most occasions defeated – all the major armies of Antiquity: Assyrians, Medes, Persians, Greeks and Macedonians. The Sarmatians, meanwhile, were among the worst enemies of the Roman Empire for several centuries. They introduced the new troop type of the heavily armoured lancer into Europe, which was soon copied by the Romans. Both the Scythians and the Sarmatians have left us many burials containing massive amounts of weapons. As a result, during past decades, it has been possible to reconstruct how they were equipped for war and which tactics they employed on the battlefield. Judging from their surviving pieces of military equipment, they had incredible metal-working capabilities and produced some of the finest weapons ever seen during Antiquity.

The historical origins of the Scythians are still a matter of debate among modern scholars, as there are no primary sources written by them detailing their own early history. Two hypotheses have emerged during recent decades, based upon different sources and evidence. The first, supported by most of the modern Russian academics, is based on what the great Greek historian Herodotus wrote about the origins of the Scythians. According to Herodotus, they were an Eastern Iranian-speaking group who settled in a geographical region known as Inner Asia, which comprised an area between present-day Turkestan and western Siberia. The second hypothesis, championed by several scholars of the Anglo-Saxon world, proposes that the Scythians emerged as a new civilization from groups belonging to a local culture that existed along the Black Sea coast (the so-called Srubna Culture). What we know for sure is that the Black Sea region, roughly corresponding to modern southern Ukraine, became the homeland of the Scythians from about 700 BC. According to Herodotus and his modern followers, the Scythians migrated to the Black Sea region from Inner Asia. However, the other hypothesis that is supported by the Anglo-Saxon scholars believes the Scythians originated in the Black Sea region as a result of the region's cultural evolution. Recent genetic studies have shown that the Scythians were strongly linked to the peoples of Inner Asia and had many elements in common with them. Consequently, it is highly probable that Herodotus's reconstruction of the early history of the Scythians is correct. During the early Iron Age, several peoples living in Inner Asia migrated across the steppes to reach southern Russia and Ukraine. These mass migrations of peoples remained a distinctive element of Inner Asia during most of Antiquity, also having enormous consequences for the history of European civilizations. Broadly speaking, the migratory movements were usually caused by the emergence of new regional powers in the steppes of Inner Asia. When a new military power emerged – this could consist of a single people or a confederation of peoples – it started to expand its territories by attacking the other steppe peoples living on its borders. If defeated in battle, the communities attacked by the emerging power had no choice but to migrate westwards in search of new lands where they could live. Moving westwards meant abandoning the heartland of the Asian steppes to enter Europe, where other civilizations had already established themselves. Around 800 BC, the Scythians were attacked in their homeland of Inner Asia by another steppe people of nomads, that of the Massagetae. The latter came to control a sizeable portion of the territory located east of the Caspian Sea and were much more numerous than the Scythians. The great military resources of the Massagetae were more than a match for the forces of the Scythians, who were forced to abandon Inner Asia due to the expansionist pressure exerted upon them. The Scythians crossed a large part of southern Russia before entering Ukraine, a region of Europe where there were all the conditions they needed to create a new Scythian homeland. Southern Ukraine had vast plains with abundant pastures for their horses and had a plentiful supply of water. This combination made it the perfect choice for a nomadic people like the Scythians, who considered horses to be their most important possessions.

When the Scythians arrived in southern Ukraine, however, the region was already inhabited by another steppe people: the Cimmerians. These had originated in Inner Asia, just like the Scythians, and migrated to the Pontic Steppe of southern Ukraine long before them. The Cimmerians are mentioned in Homer's *Odyssey* and thus already had contact with the Greek world as far back as the ninth century BC. The Ukrainian homeland of the Cimmerians extended from the high mountains of the Caucasus to the coastline of Crimea. According to Herodotus, the Cimmerians had submitted the original local inhabitants of southern Ukraine and absorbed them into their own people. Indeed, within Cimmerian society there was a clear division between the so-called 'royal race' that descended from the original Cimmerians and the inferior 'common race' descended from the native inhabitants of pre-Cimmerian southern Ukraine. When the Scythians invaded the Pontic Steppe, several major battles took place between the newcomers and the Cimmerians. Due to the lack of written sources, we know practically nothing of this conflict, which probably lasted for a few decades. What we do know, however, is that the Scythians prevailed and expelled the Cimmerians from southern Ukraine. The Scythians thereafter settled in the region and started to dominate the Pontic Steppe.

The Greeks, starting from the seventh century BC, began founding several colonies on the Crimean coastline of the Black Sea. These small centres, initially created just to act as commercial outposts, were soon transformed into large and rich cities that controlled the trade routes of the northern Black Sea. The Greek colonies of Crimea, in particular, became fundamental in the development of strong commercial relations

Scythian horse archer. (*Photo by Jasmin Parvanov, copyright by Equestrian Martial Arts School – Madara Horseman, Obzor, Bulgaria; Bulgarian School of Ancient Military Arts – Greatness, Varna, Bulgaria; Association for Restoration and Preservation of Bulgarian Traditions – Avitohol, Varna, Bulgaria*)

between the Scythians and the Greek world. Thanks to massive exports of wheat and grain, the Greek colonies of Crimea flourished and became increasingly important politically. The Greek merchants were very interested in trading with the Scythians, as southern Ukraine produced large amounts of grain (badly needed in Greece) and was rich in natural resources such as gold or silver. The Scythians, meanwhile, wanted to purchase luxury goods from Greek merchants selling wine, oil, vases, clothes and jewels. The Greek presence on the Ukrainian coastline did not represent a threat to the Scythians, who maintained peaceful relations with the Greeks for several centuries. Small-scale wars occasionally broke out between a Greek colony and a Scythian community, but these never lasted long and resulted in few casualties on either side. The Greeks were too few to venture into the interior of Ukraine, while the Scythians were not capable of conducting siege operations to conquer a Greek colony. As a result, although the Greeks sometimes perceived the Scythians as a potential menace, in practice they never ran the risk of being expelled from their flourishing coastal cities.

By the time of Alexander the Great's ascendancy to the throne, the Scythians had a long border in common with the expanding Kingdom of Macedonia, which by then dominated most of the Balkans. The northern border between the Macedonian territories in Thrace and those of the Scythians, marked by the Danube River, became an unstable one after Alexander and his Macedonian army left Europe to invade the Persian Empire in Asia. The Scythians took advantage of the Macedonians' temporary local weakness to launch several devastating incursions across Thrace. The Macedonians, however, responded by organizing a large-scale invasion of Scythia, for which they assembled an army of 30,000 soldiers. These were commanded by Zopyrion, an experienced general who was the governor of Thrace when the expedition was launched in 331 BC. Ancient sources provide scant detail of the Macedonian invasion of Scythia, but it is known that the Scythians employed an effective scorched earth strategy to slow down their advance. The Macedonians were unable to engage the Scythians in a pitched battle, but did advance deep into southern Ukraine. Zopyrion's objective was to reach the Greek colonies in Ukraine, probably with the intention of annexing them to Macedonia and using their ports to receive supplies. At some point, however, the Macedonians were surrounded by a massive Scythian army. The ensuing clash was probably the worst military disaster suffered by the Macedonians, with Zopyrion and all his 30,000 soldiers being massacred by the Scythians. We have no idea how the encounter developed, even if it was an ambush or a pitched battle. Nevertheless, it is reasonable to suppose that the Macedonian phalangites were overcome on open terrain by the superior cavalry of their enemy.

The origins of the Sarmatians are, like those of the Scythians, controversial because no written primary sources created by the Sarmatians exist. What is known, however, is that the early Sarmatian culture had a lot in common with that of the Saka (called Eastern Scythians or Asiatic Scythians by several contemporary Greek historians). The Sarmatians consisted of several different tribes and, compared with the Scythians, were more fragmented from a political point of view. The earliest

Scythian archer. (*Photo and copyright by Scythian State*)

Sarmatian community recorded in the works of the Greek authors was that of the Sauromates, who probably gave their name to all the Sarmatian peoples. The Sauromates lived on the eastern bank of the Don River in the sixth century BC and were strongly linked to the Scythians, speaking a corrupted form of the Scythian language. When the Persian monarch, Darius I, attacked Scythia in 513 BC, the Sauromates joined forces with the Scythians and sent various military contingents to Ukraine in order to fight against the Persian troops. By the end of the fifth century BC, the Sauromates had disappeared from history, having probably been absorbed by the Scythians or contributing to the formation of the later Sarmatian groups. During the closing decades of the fifth century BC, a new Sarmatian tribe, that of the Siraces, migrated from present-day Kazakhstan to the Don River region of southern Russia. The Siraces established their homeland north of Scythia but gradually expelled the Scythians from the interior areas of the Caucasus. Here, they met for the first time the Greeks living in the colonies around the Black Sea, with whom they established commercial relations. Around 120 BC, another two Sarmatian tribes – the Iazyges and Roxolani – started to be mentioned in contemporary written sources compiled by Greek or Roman authors. These tribes roamed across southern Ukraine, defeating the Scythians on several occasions and conquering their homeland. The Iazyges and Roxolani came from the heart of the Eurasian steppes and thus looked much more 'barbarian' to the contemporary Greek and Roman observers than the Scythians.

The Iazyges later established their homeland in modern-day Hungary, between the Danube and Tisza rivers, whereas the Roxolani settled north of the lower Danube. From the early decades of the first century AD, the history of both these Sarmatian tribes became strongly linked with that of the Dacians, who lived south of the Danube. Following the end of the Dacian Wars fought by the Roman Emperor Trajan from AD 101–106 and the Roman conquest of Dacia, the Roxolani and Iazyges fought a series of wars between themselves and thereby became increasingly weaker militarily. Between AD 236 and 305, the Iazyges launched a series of incursions against the Roman provinces in the Balkans, obtaining some minor successes. On several occasions, however, they were defeated by the Roman emperors facing them. After the Goths began migrating across Eastern Europe, the Romans allowed thousands of Sarmatians to settle on the territories of the Empire as *foederati*, or allies. The Romans greatly appreciated the quality of the Sarmatian heavy cavalry and always tried to include large numbers of them in their military forces. By settling the Sarmatian tribes on the frontier areas of the Empire, the Romans could also count on some excellent military contingents tasked with defending the imperial borders from Germanic incursions. Many Sarmatian aristocrats obtained Roman citizenship and several Sarmatian colonies were created across the Roman Empire (even far from the frontier areas). The

Scythian archer. (*Photo and copyright by Amages Drachen*)

ascendancy of the Goths in Eastern Europe had extremely negative consequences for the Sarmatians, who were defeated on several occasions by the powerful Germanic warriors. The Sarmatian tribes also came under attack from another people of the steppes: the Alans, who probably originated from the fusion of some eastern Sarmatian groups with those of the Massagetae. The Alans, after entering the Pontic Steppe, soon became the dominant military power of the region and replaced the Sarmatians, exactly as the latter had done with the Scythians. Pressed by the superior numbers of the Goths and the Alans, the Sarmatians had no choice but to migrate inside the Roman Empire. A great number of Sarmatian warriors then enlisted in the Roman Army, while most of the Sarmatian civilians sought refuge in Thrace and Macedonia. By AD 400, the Sarmatians had mostly been absorbed by the Roman Empire, except for a few communities that became part of the Alans. With the ascendancy of the Huns in the early fifth century AD, both the Alans and the Goths lost their prominence in the Pontic Steppe and became vassals of the Hunnic Empire.

The military forces of the Scythians, like those of all the other nomadic peoples of the Eurasian steppes, mostly consisted of cavalry. Indeed, the Scythians were acknowledged as the best horse-breeders of the world during Antiquity. It is important to note, however, that Scythian armies included sizeable infantry contingents too, comprising the poorest individuals from each tribal group. The Greek historians Herodotus and Thucydides described the Scythian armed forces as large contingents of mounted archers, while Diodorus Siculus referred to battles that saw the participation of large contingents of Scythian infantry. According to the latest research, it seems that the balance between cavalry and infantry within the Scythian military changed considerably over the centuries. When the Scythians migrated to the Pontic Steppe, their armies were large cavalry forces. During their early settlement in Ukraine, the Scythians were a people on the move and still had all the distinctive features of the nomadic peoples of Eurasia. They had no permanent settlements and did not practice agriculture, instead moving across the vast plains of the steppe with their horses and cattle, building seasonal camps and following the natural cycles. Over time, however, the Scythians mixed with the local inhabitants of southern Ukraine and formed several new communities that were partially 'Hellenized'. As a result of this, some Scythian groups began building permanent settlements and started to practice agriculture. It was from these new communities that the large infantry contingents described by Diodorus Siculus came. The early Scythian armies also comprised some foot contingents, which were provided by the sedentary peoples living in Ukraine. These had been transformed into vassals of the nomadic Scythians after they had occupied the Pontic Steppe, and as such were required to provide auxiliary contingents.

The formidable Scythian cavalry had two main components: horse archers and heavy horsemen. The horse archers were much more numerous than the heavy cavalrymen, since every able-bodied Scythian male was capable of fighting as a mounted archer. They wore no armour and were equipped with the deadly composite bow of the Eurasian steppes. Whereas the common Scythian people made up the light cavalry of the horse archers, the heavy cavalry consisted of noble professional warriors who were rich enough to equip themselves with full armour. Broadly speaking, each heavy cavalry contingent was commanded by a prince and consisted of his armed retinue. The professional warriors of the heavy cavalry were used to fight in formation and were thus more disciplined than the horse archers, acting as elite shock troops. Scythian battle tactics were quite simple but worked extremely well in the steppes, having evolved from the movements made by the Scythians while governing their herds of horses and cattle over vast plains. These movements had one main objective: concentrating the dispersed animals at a single point of the steppe in order to move them towards new areas of pasture. The battles of the steppe peoples were extremely rapid and violent, beginning with massive attacks by the horse archers, who concentrated their volleys on the flanks of the enemy in order to oblige them to concentrate their forces in the centre. When the enemies had been herded into a single point of the battlefield, the heavily armoured cavalry launched a decisive frontal charge that usually won the day. These tactics worked perfectly against enemies having cavalry armies, but were not always effective when their opponents could deploy large heavy infantry contingents (like the Greek hoplites, Macedonian phalangites or Roman legionaries). The Scythian cavalry was famous for its great tactical flexibility: it was capable of regrouping in the thick of the action and of changing direction very rapidly in order to strike where needed. When the enemy formations had been broken by the heavy cavalry, the horse archers pursued the defeated enemies in order to transform their retreat into a rout.

Scythian dead were buried in barrow-mounds known as kurgans, and each Scythian warrior was accompanied on his journey into eternity by the possessions that were most important to him in life. These included his weapons, meaning that thanks to the rich finds of military equipment that have emerged from the excavations of Scythian barrows, it is possible to have a very clear picture of what Scythian armour and offensive weapons looked like. The grave of a common warrior, who had fought as a horse archer during his life, usually contained just a few elements: a composite bow, several dozen arrows and a couple of spears. The tombs of nobles and kings, instead, included whole arsenals of top-quality weapons: armour, helmets, swords, quivers full of arrows, dozens of spears and horse skeletons with full military harness. The standard type of armour worn by most of the Scythian warriors consisted of

Scythian archer. Note the complex decorations of both the clothing and the equipment.
(*Photo and copyright by Amages Drachen*)

flexible leather corselets that were partly or entirely covered with overlapping scales of bronze or iron. The Scythians were masters at producing bronze scale armour and did not cover only their leather corselets with metal scales; their helmets and shields were also frequently reinforced by applying bronze or iron scales on their outer surfaces. Scythian armourers cut the scales from sheet metal with a pointed tool or shears; the scales were then attached to the soft leather base of the corselets by thin leather thongs or animal tendons. Each individual scale was set in such a way that it covered between a third and half of the width of the next scale sideways. Each row of scales overlapped the one placed below it, protecting the stitching where it was exposed in holes through the metal. Despite providing excellent protection to their wearers, the corselets did not significantly hinder the movements of a mounted warrior. Various types of corselets were used, according to the economic capabilities of their wearers: the simplest and cheapest ones had metal scales only around the neck and upper breast or on the front surface. Short-sleeved corselets were worn by the common warriors, while the nobles often had long-sleeved corselets. Quite frequently, a doubled yoke of scale-work was applied across the upper back and extending forward over the shoulders to the sides of the breast, in order to offer better protection for the shoulders. The scales of a corselet were sometimes made from two different materials, in order for the wearer to look even more magnificent.

The early helmets of the Scythians were of the Kuban type, being heavy cast-bronze helmets, fitting tightly to the skull and protecting the face by means of cheek-pieces that left cut-outs for the eyes. From the fifth century BC, the Kuban helmet started to be replaced by the new Phrygian helmet, a forward-pointing Phrygian cap made of leather and covered with metal scales. The Phrygian cap was extremely popular in the Balkans and was worn by most of the Thracian tribes, so it is highly probable that the Scythians started wearing it after coming into contact with them. The Phrygian helmets could have cheek-pieces and neck-guards, always made of leather covered with metal scales. Being easy and cheap to produce, the Phrygian helmets were used also by the majority of the Scythian common warriors. Over time, Scythian noblemen started to purchase large numbers of bronze helmets from the merchants of the Greek colonies in Crimea. These helmets, according to recent findings, were mostly worn by the Scythian heavy cavalry and could be of the following Hellenic models: Corinthian, Chalcidian or Attic. The defensive equipment of a Scythian noble warrior often included leg protectors, which could be made of leather covered with scales or consist of bronze greaves purchased in the Greek colonies of Crimea. Leggings covered with bronze or iron scales were a distinctive element of the Scythian heavy cavalry's panoply. The Greek-style bronze greaves of the richest warriors could be gilded and have decorative incisions. Both the helmets and the greaves purchased

Scythian archer. (*Photo and copyright by Amages Drachen*)

from the Greek merchants were part of the hoplites' heavy infantry equipment; the Scythians, however, adapted them to their traditional defensive panoply. The poorest Scythian warriors, fighting as light horsemen or light infantrymen, had simple shields made from woven willow. The noble warriors, however, had massive shields faced with iron. These were constructed with a wooden base that was covered with scales of iron, which were sewn to each other and to the backing with wire. Kings and princes occasionally had shields covered with a single iron plate, being decorated with applied motifs obtained from other metals. Deer and panthers were among the wild animals more frequently represented in Scythian decorations. Scythian shields were usually rectangular with curved angles, but could sometimes be crescent-shaped like those of the Thracians. The poorest Scythian warriors, especially those serving as light infantrymen, wore only a girdle for protection of their body. This was made of leather covered with metal scales, being broad enough to cover the whole abdomen. The armour worn by the horses of the Scythian heavy cavalry evolved considerably across the centuries. Initially, it consisted just of metal plates and pendant decorations attached to the bridle for protection of the horse's head, but pieces of leather horse-cloth covered with metal scales were later introduced and became increasingly popular. A thick felt apron for the horse's breast was also developed in order to provide better protection against enemy arrows. The Scythians, like all the other steppe peoples of Antiquity, rode without stirrups but were masters in the production of effective bridles. These were often decorated with bronze discs or plates. Scythian saddles were quite flat and simple, being made from leather.

Every Scythian man had a composite bow and arrows, the bow being the traditional weapon of the Scythians and all the nomadic warriors of the steppes. Contemporary written sources describe the Scythian composite bows as being unstrung and recurved, their overall shape resembling that of the Greek letter *sigma* or the crescent moon, with both ends curved inwards. The Scythian bow was quite short – 80cm – but extremely powerful thanks to its composite construction. The composite bow was made from horn, wood and sinew, which were laminated together. The horn was on the belly facing the archer, while sinew was on the outer side of the wooden core. The wooden core gave the bow its shape and dimensional stability. When the bow was drawn, the sinew (stretched on the outside) and horn (compressed on the inside) stored more energy than the wood for the same length of bow. The construction of a composite bow was a very complex process, requiring more varieties of material than a wooden bow and much more time. A composite bow was often made of multiple pieces, joined with animal glue in V-splices. Such a construction allowed the use of woods with different mechanical properties for the bending and non-bending sections: the wood of the bending part of the limb had to endure intense shearing stress. A thin layer of horn was glued onto what would be the belly of the bow, which could store more energy than wood in compression. Goat and sheep horn was commonly used for this purpose. The sinew, soaked in animal glue, was then laid in layers on the back of the bow, the strands of sinew oriented along the length of the bow. The sinew was normally obtained from the lower legs and back of wild deer or domestic ungulates. Sinew would extend much more than wood, again allowing more energy storage. Hide glue was used to attach layers of sinew to the back of the bow and the horn belly to the wooden core. The animal glue could lose strength in humid conditions and be quickly ruined by rain or submersion in water, so composite bows were always stored in protective leather cases. Historically, peoples living in humid or rainy regions have favoured wooden bows, while those who settled in dry or arid regions have preferred composite ones. The main advantage of composite bows over longbows was their combination of smaller size with high power. Composite bows were recurved, as their shape curved away from the archer, a design that gavs them higher draw-weight in the early stages of the archer's draw, therby storing more total energy. The string of the Scythian bows was made from horsehair or animal tendon. Each bow was carried in a special leather case slung from the waistbelt. This case, known as a *gorytos* and often covered externally with metal plates, also contained up to seventy-five arrows. It thus served both as a case for the bow and a quiver for the arrows. The shaft of the arrows was omade from reed or a thin birch branch. The stabilizing fletching was made from birds' feathers. The heads of the arrows could be of bronze or iron, and had different shapes according to the use that the archer had for them. The standard arrows used for fighting had trilobate heads that were capable of piercing enemy armour from long distances thanks to their excellent aerodynamic form. Scythian archers were capable of firing between ten and twelve arrows in a minute and to hit a target some 500 metres away.

The earliest Scythian swords derived from those used by the Cimmerians, with a two-edged and almost parallel-sided blade tapering at the point. The blade was 60–70cm long. Daggers, having the same basic features and being employed as secondary weapons, had blades 35–40cm in length. The early Scythian swords were decorated with thin gold plates fixed around the hilt. Scythian swords gradually changed the shape of their blades, which became that of an elongated isosceles triangle with a continuous taper down its whole length. During the fourth century BC, single-edged versions of this new kind of blade started to be produced. The pommel of the Scythian swords, which had a simple crossbar shape in the early types, gradually changed to be more complex, with two talons of iron rising and curling inwards. The grip, initially having a cylindrical shape, gradually came to have a double-tapered or oval shape that proved very practical for combat use. The guard evolved to have

Scythian archer. War hammers and short axes were popular secondary weapons among the Scythians. (*Photo and copyright by Amages Drachen*)

Scythian archer fixing the string of his composite bow. (*Photo by Jasmin Parvanov, copyright by Equestrian Martial Arts School – Madara Horseman, Obzor, Bulgaria; Bulgarian School of Ancient Military Arts – Greatness, Varna, Bulgaria; Association for Restoration and Preservation of Bulgarian Traditions – Avitohol, Varna, Bulgaria*)

a triangular shape, with a sharp and curved indent in the centre of its bottom edge. The scabbards of the Scythian swords were made of wood covered with leather and hung from the waistbelt by a thong passing through its projecting 'ear'. Swords had a very important religious function among the Scythians, who frequently built ceremonial altars in the steppe that had a single sacred sword placed on top of them. As a result, they were respected as a noble weapon that was passed from father to son. The Scythian horsemen used different kinds of spears, according to the tactical function that they had to perform on the battlefield. The heavy cavalrymen were equipped with long spears of the *kontus* type. This was about 4 metres long and had to be wielded with two hands while directing the horse using the knees, making it a specialist weapon that required a lot of training and good horsemanship to use. The *kontus* was reputedly a weapon of great power compared to other cavalry spears of the time. The great length of this deadly weapon was probably the origin of its name, since the Greek word *kontus* meant 'oar' or 'barge-pole'. The heavy cavalrymen who formed the personal retinue of a Scythian prince and wore full armour were usually armed with the *kontus*, which was employed as a shock weapon during frontal charges. Shorter spears, about 1.7–1.8 metres long, were used for throwing and thrusting by both Scythian cavalrymen and infantrymen. These weapons had leaf-shaped heads with a central spine, as well as a socket for the wooden shaft. Scythian light cavalrymen and light infantrymen carried throwing javelins instead of spears. These had an iron shank with a small pyramidal head, which was sharply barbed and designed to pierce enemy shield. In addition to swords, the Scythians employed other weapons for hand-to-hand fighting: battleaxes and maces. Battleaxes had iron blades that could be richly decorated, while maces had lobed heads and were also used as symbols of authority.

Differently from the Scythians, Sarmatian armies consisted almost entirely of cavalry as none of the Sarmatian tribes were ever fully Hellenized like some of the Scythians were. As was the case with all the peoples of the steppes, each able-bodied Sarmatian male was a warrior and was expected to fight under the guidance of his tribal leader. Like with the Scythians, the poorest individuals of the Sarmatian communities served as horse archers, while the richest ones made up a military caste of professional warriors who were equipped as heavy cavalrymen and comprised the personal retinues of the various noble warlords. The professional warriors belonging to the same retinue were linked by strong personal bonds. They swore oaths of friendship and loyalty to each other, which were sealed during special ceremonies by drinking drops of each other's blood mixed with wine. The early Sarmatian armies, like the Scythian ones, were largely horse archers, acting as auxiliaries for an elite minority of heavily armoured cavalrymen, so their battlefield tactics were exactly the same as those employed by the Scythians. Over time, however, a crucial evolutionary process took place within the Sarmatian mounted forces. Frequently being forced to face the Roman legions, they started to modify their internal balance between horse archers and heavy cavalrymen. Combat experiences showed that mounted archers had great difficulties in defeating a Roman heavy infantry force. The Sarmatian heavy cavalrymen, however, often achieved decisive victories over the Roman legions thanks to the deadly impact of their frontal charges. Consequently, the number of horse archers in the Sarmatian armies decreased considerably, while the importance of the heavy contingents consisting of professional fighters was greatly augmented. The Sarmatians are often lauded as having invented a new form of 'super-heavy' cavalry, known as cataphracts by the Greeks (the term meaning 'covered with armour'). Cataphracts were basically horsemen covered in full armour who rode a similarly fully armoured horse. Equipped with the heavy *kontus* lance, they were capable of crushing any heavy infantry contingent deployed by their enemy. According to ancient sources, this new troop type of armoured lancers was invented by the Sarmatians, but in reality cataphracts were only imported into Europe by them from the Asian regions of Bactria and Sogdia, where they had originated among the Sakas during the fifth century BC. The great Roman historian Tacitus was the first ancient writer to describe in full detail the distinctive panoply of the Sarmatian cataphracts. Despite wearing super-heavy equipment, they were extremely flexible tactically and could perform effective feigned retreats. Like the Scythians, the Sarmatians could also count on lightly armed infantry contingents provided by the local communities of Ukraine and southern Russia that had been submitted by them. These, however, only performed auxiliary military duties of little importance.

The early Sarmatian heavy cavalry was mostly equipped with corselets made of leather and covered with leather scales, but corselets with bronze or iron scales almost identical to those worn by the Scythians eventually came into standard use. Noble and professional warriors wore corselets entirely covered with metal scales, while the common soldiers usually had only some bronze or iron plates applied on key points of their leather corselets. The corselets, when covered with scales, usually reached the mid-thigh and had a slit at each side extending up to the waistbelt in order to facilitate riding. A leather belt secured the cuirass high around the waist, taking much of its weight off the shoulders. According to the most recent findings, the Sarmatian corselets mostly had iron scales, as bronze became less popular from the first century AD. With the progression of time, especially during the period of the Dacian Wars, many Sarmatian heavy horsemen started to replace their scale armour with chainmail cuirasses, but these were quite difficult and costly to produce. As an alternative, the poorest warriors could wear leather corselets covered with scales made

Scythian light cavalryman equipped with a spear and throwing javelin.
(*Photo and copyright by Scythian State*)

Sarmatian heavy cavalryman equipped with a spear and composite bow. (*Photo and copyright by Amages Drachen*)

from horn or horse hooves. According to ancient sources, the Sarmatians experienced serious difficulties in finding enough iron to produce their military equipment after the Romans conquered Dacia, and henceforth had to start using alternative materials for the scales of their cuirasses. During the early decades of their presence in the Pontic Steppe, the Sarmatians wore Greek-style helmets mostly produced in the Hellenic colonies. These – of the Corinthian, Chalcidian and Attic models – were sometimes modified by the Sarmatians, who cut away their lower parts to improve vision. The Sarmatians also employed Celtic Montefortino helmets, which they bought or copied from the Bastarnae Celtic communities living in the northern Balkans. Over time, however, a new kind of helmet replaced all the previous models employed by the Sarmatians: the spangenhelm. This term is clearly of Germanic origin: 'spangen' refers to the metal strips that formed the framework of the helmet, while 'helm' simply means helmet. The characteristic metal strips of a spangenhelm connected between three and six steel or bronze plates, which made up a framework in a conical design, curving with the shape of the head and culminating in a point. The front of the helmet generally included a nasal. Spangenhelms could also incorporate chainmail as neck protection, forming a sort of aventail on the back. Some surviving examples also include eye protection, having a shape that resembles modern eyeglass frames; others include a full face mask. Older spangenhelms often had cheek flaps made from metal or leather. In general terms, the spangenhelm offered effective protection for the head and was relatively easy and cheap to produce. The defensive equipment of the Sarmatian heavy cavalrymen was completed by the shield, which was made of wood covered with metal scales exactly like the standard shield employed by most of the Scythian warriors. Once the Sarmatian heavy cavalrymen were re-equipped as cataphracts and adopted the *kontus* as their main offensive weapon, however, shields ceased to be a component of the Sarmatians' usual panoply. However, light cavalry and infantry continued to carry simple wicker shields until the Sarmatians disappeared from history.

The main offensive weapon of the Sarmatian heavy cavalry, the *kontus*, was held two-handed: the left arm aimed and supported the weapon's weight while the right arm thrust it from the hip. The main offensive weapon of the Sarmatian mounted archers was the composite bow, which had all the same features as the Scythian composite bow. From the fourth century BC, this design was improved thanks to the addition of bone laths at the grip and 'ears' (ends), which gave additional power to the weapon. The Sarmatians also employed the Scythian *gorytos* to hold the bow and its arrows. During the first century AD, the Sarmatians began using a new, larger model of composite bow, which was probably designed by the Hunnic tribes and was thus known as a Hunnish bow. This measured 120cm in length, which made it much more powerful than the Scythian bow. Indeed, it was probably the adoption of this new type of bow that determined the victory of the Sarmatians in their battles fought on the Pontic Steppe against the Scythians. The Hunnish bow was usually asymmetrical in shape, with the top half above the grip being longer. It was too big to be carried in the traditional *gorytos*, so the Sarmatians had to design a new soft bow case for it. Arrows were carried in two tall cylindrical quivers, which were made of deerskin leather. The early Sarmatians had long swords very similar to those carried by the Scythians, but with an antennae-shaped pommel in the Celtic fashion. These were progressively replaced by new swords that had a ring-shaped pommel, which could be produced in a long version (70–130cm) or a short one (60–70cm). The short swords were carried in scabbards secured via two pairs of wings by leather straps that passed around the right thigh, while the longer ones were carried on the left side in conventional scabbards. Sarmatian warriors often had both a long sword employed for cavalry fighting and a short sword for use in hand-to-hand fighting. Like most of the nomadic peoples of the steppes, the Scythians and the Sarmatians were experts in the use of the lasso, which was used while moving cattle from one place to another but could also become a weapon. The Sarmatians, according to ancient sources, were capable of tossing the lasso over an enemy's neck to pull him down from his horse. The horse armour used by the Sarmatian cataphracts consisted of full bards covered with leather or iron scales. Sarmatian saddles, differently from Scythian ones, had four 'horns' at their angles, which gave much greater stability to an armoured lancer while charging thanks to their ergonomic shape. The Sarmatians were the inventors of the draco standard, which was later adopted by the cavalry of the Roman Army. As is suggested by its name, this had the form of a dragon, with open wolf-like jaws containing several metal tongues. The hollow head of the dragon was made of metal and was mounted on a pole, with a long fabric tube fixed to the rear. When used, the draco was held aloft, where it filled with air and made a shrill sound as the wind passed through its metal tongues. It was an early example of psychological warfare, and was especially used during the opening phases of a pitched battle. The wind-sock standard, however, also had another important function in steppe warfare, providing evidence of the wind direction to help archers in their aim during pitched clashes.

Sarmatian archer. (*Photo and copyright by Amages Drachen*)

Sarmatian warrior throwing his lasso, an extremely popular weapon among the steppe peoples. (*Photo and copyright by Amages Drachen*)

Chapter 2

The Huns of Attila, 376–470

The historical origins of the Huns, probably – along with the Mongols – the most famous steppe people of history, are mysterious and extremely controversial. After many studies, conducted using various approaches, most contemporary scholars now consider the Huns to be the direct heirs of a powerful nomadic population originating from Mongolia: the Xiongnu. These people developed in the Mongolian Plateau during the third century BC and gradually became a major military power in Asia, especially after they began invading the North China Plain that is crossed by the Yellow River. For centuries, the nomadic Xiongnu and the Chinese Empire of the Han Dynasty fought in a huge clash of civilizations, during which the survival of the Chinese Empire was threatened by the expansionism of the Xiongnu. The latter, differently from the other steppe peoples who had preceded them, did not expand westwards in search of new lands but eastwards. This led to them clashing with the powerful Han Empire, which had its heartland in the fertile North China Plain. Between 133 BC and AD 91, the Xiongnu and the Chinese were continuously at war, in a conflict that saw victories and defeats on both sides. Eventually, after the Han Army obtained a decisive victory at the Battle of Yiwulu in AD 73, the Xiongnu were crushed. The Chinese had learned from their early defeats and began to adopt some features of their enemy's troops – such as the extensive use of mounted archers and armoured heavy cavalrymen – for their own armies. After their defeat, the southern communities of the Xiongnu became semi-autonomous vassals of the Han Empire, but those in the north were forced to migrate from their homeland and moved to the area around Lake Balkhash (located on the modern border between Kazakhstan and China). It was from these groups of exiles that the Huns probably originated, since both Chinese and Indian contemporary sources use the terms 'Xiongnu' and 'Huns' to refer to them.

Around AD 370, some of the Huns began migrating westwards – probably due to climate changes taking place in the steppes of Central Asia – and started invading the Pontic Steppe of modern Ukraine. This region, as we have already seen, was inhabited by the Germanic Goths who had defeated the nomadic Sarmatians just a few decades before. The arrival of the Huns caused a political and military revolution in Eastern Europe, their superior weapons and tactics enabling them to inflict a

Hun heavy cavalryman; note the
complexity of the composite armour.
(*Colour plate by Patricio Greve Moller,
copyright by Gabriele Esposito*)

series of humiliating defeats on the Goths. The Goths were left with no choice but to become tributary vassals of the Huns or to migrate into the Roman Empire as refugees by crossing the course of the Lower Danube. In AD 376, thousands of Goths entered Roman territory, causing a sudden collapse of the imperial defences. Two years later, in AD 378, the Roman Army was crushed by the migrating Germanic warriors in the Battle of Adrianople. This clash marked the beginning of the 'barbarian invasions' for the Roman Empire and was of enormous historical importance. The Huns, with their migration towards the Pontic Steppe, had initiated a series of gigantic movements of people that – in the long run – would cause the fall of the Western Roman Empire. In AD 395, after having secured control over most of the Germanic peoples living in Eastern Europe, the Huns started attacking the eastern provinces of the Roman Empire with a series of devastating raids. They struck first in Thrace, after crossing the Danube and overrunning a large portion of the Balkans. Then, coming from the Caucasus, they overran Armenia and pillaged Cappadocia. Thanks to the geographical position of their new homeland, the Huns could attack the Roman Empire both along the western coastline of the Black Sea in the Balkans and along its eastern shores from the Caucasus. The highly mobile cavalry armies of the Huns entered Syria and threatened the rich city of Antioch, an event that shocked the Romans, who were not prepared to face such a large-scale incursion of a nomadic people. In the Middle East, meanwhile, the Huns raided the territory of the Sasanian Empire, which was the main power in the region. The nomads came close to the Sasanian capital of Ctesiphon, but were driven back by an effective counter-attack. The Sasanians deployed large Iranian-style military forces that had a lot in common with those of the Huns, including horse archers and heavy cavalry.

In AD 408, under the leadership of Uldin – who is the first Hun chief to be identified by name in the contemporary sources – the Huns crossed the Danube in great numbers and pillaged Thrace. By that time, the Western Roman Empire and Eastern Roman Empire had become separate political entities, so the Eastern Romans had to face the invading nomads alone. The Roman authorities were able to stop the Hunnic incursions into the Balkans, at least temporarily, by paying large sums of money to Uldin's warriors. Many of these warriors deserted and the Hunnic leader was forced to return to his territories located north of the Danube (after which he is not mentioned again in any of the surviving sources). It soon became clear, however, that the Huns were interested in conquering large parts of the Roman Empire, in particular the vast plains of Pannonia (modern Hungary). By establishing military bases in Pannonia, the Huns could invade any province of the Eastern or Western Empire. The Roman military commanders, after a few encounters with the Huns, soon realized that their enemies had exceptional combat capabilities thanks to the great mobility and tactical flexibility of their mounted contingents. The first senior Roman officer who correctly identified the military potential of the Huns was Flavius Aetius, the *magister militum* (i.e. overall commander) of the Western Empire's armies. By the 430s, the Western Empire was extremely weak militarily, its territory having been ravaged for decades by migrating Germanic communities and its troops shattered by several significant defeats. Most of the Roman military forces, at least in the western provinces, consisted of foreign mercenaries who were paid for their services and were loyal only to their employees, provided that these had enough money to do so. Flavius Aetius was one of the many warlords who emerged in the Western Empire during the turbulent fifth century AD, his personal capabilities allowing him to assume a prominent politico-military role and control a substantial number of effective troops. These fighters included many Germanic professional soldiers, as well as a significant number of Hun mercenaries. In 425, thanks to the positive relations that he had with some of their leaders, Flavius Aetius was able to recruit an entire army of Huns and lead them into Italy.

The friendship of Flavius Aetius with the Huns made him the most powerful man in the Western Empire. During this period, the political power of the Roman state was in the hands of Empress Galla Placidia and her son, Valentinian III. Galla Placidia was highly intelligent and had great political experience, while her Valentinian III had significant mental problems. Initially, the imperial court, based at Ravenna in northern Italy, considered Flavius Aetius a potential rival and tried to limit his military power. However, Galla Placidia eventually had to accept that Flavius Aetius was the only leader who could assemble and guide the military forces needed to face the Germanic invaders. In 433, the *magister militum*, who was specifically responsible for the defence of Gaul, signed an agreement with the Huns according to which some parts of Pannonia (located along the Sava River) were to be ceded to the nomads. Flavius Aetius signed the agreement with Rugila, a powerful warlord who had become the overall ruler of the Huns living on the borders of the Western Empire. In 434, however, Rugila died and was succeeded by the two young sons of his brother, Mundzuk: Bleda and Attila. Both these youngsters were extremely ambitious, but they had very different ideas about how to cause the collapse of the Western Empire. Bleda wanted to continue the policy of Rugila by signing new treaties with the Roman authorities that were extremely positive for the Huns. He was convinced that the Romans would cede to him rich territories and large sums of money in exchange for the Huns' promise of defending the imperial lands from Germanic invasions. Attila, instead, had full confidence in the military superiority of his warriors and wanted to conquer the Western Empire with a large-scale invasion. Initially, Bleda's political vision prevailed; Bleda was also older than Attila and

Hun heavy cavalryman equipped with a full set of lamellar armour.
(*Photo by Csongrádi Turán HSE, copyright by Hungarian Turan Foundation, Tamás Horváth*)

thus had more authority among the Huns. They negotiated a new and extremely favourable treaty with the Eastern Empire, according to which the Romans were to pay a tribute of 700 pounds of gold to the Huns every year, as well as to open all their markets to Hun traders and pay a ransom for each Roman citizen taken prisoner by the nomads.

After signing the new treaty, the Huns did not attack any Roman territories for around five years and used the large sums of money paid by the Romans to strengthen their military forces. They tried to invade the Sasanian Empire in order to obtain the payment of a further tribute, but their campaign ended in failure when they were defeated in Armenia after having crossed the Caucasus. In 440, the Huns reappeared on the borders of Pannonia and conducted a raid against the Roman markets that were established on the northern bank of the Danube (which had the specific task of trading with the Huns). After killing several Roman merchants, by using as a pretext the desecration of some of their religious sites by a Roman bishop, the Huns crossed the Danube and attacked the Roman province of Illyria. They advanced with spectacular speed and conquered many cities, aided by the Eastern Empire having failed to reinforce its military defences in the northern Balkans in recent years. The Romans, convinced that the Huns had been fully satisfied by the signing of the treaty that had been agreed a few years before, focused all their attention on the Germanic peoples instead of preparing for a Hun invasion. Bleda and Attila devastated the Balkans during 441, conquering Singidunum (modern Belgrade) and the large city of Sirmium. After a long pause that lasted for most of the year 442, they resumed their offensive by besieging Naissus (this was the first occasion that the Huns built some rudimentary siege engines) and sacking several Roman military bases. In just a few months they reached the outskirts of Constantinople, the rich capital of the Eastern Empire, where they routed a large Roman force that had been assembled to stop them. At this point, however, the Huns could not besiege Constantinople due to their lack of siege equipment capable of breaking through the city's massive walls, which had been recently reinforced. The Romans, having no forces left to expel the Huns from the Balkans, had no choice but to negotiate with the nomads. New peace terms were agreed, which were harsher than those contained in the previous treaty: the Eastern Empire agreed to hand over 6,000 Roman pounds of gold to the Huns, the annual tribute paid by the Roman authorities was tripled and the ransom for each Roman prisoner was increased. In the long-run, such terms could have caused the complete financial collapse of the Eastern Empire.

Having left the Balkans, Attila and Bleda went back to the plains of Pannonia to reorganize their forces. They had obtained a spectacular success, but their political visions were becoming increasingly divergent. Bleda was satisfied with what had been obtained from the Eastern Empire and had no intention of attacking the Western Empire (at least for a few years), whereas Attila was determined to invest Gaul with all his strength before the Romans could recover from their recent defeats. Around 445, a power struggle began among the Huns, both Bleda and Attila gathering considerable numbers of supporters. In the end it was Attila who prevailed, since

Hun heavy cavalryman armed with a sword.
(*Photo by Csongrádi Turán HSE, copyright by Hungarian Turan Foundation, Tamás Horváth*)

the majority of the Huns wanted to continue raiding the rich Roman provinces and were not interested in living peacefully. Bleda vehemently opposed his brother until he was assassinated by Attila. There are very few surviving details about this important episode, but it seems that Attila killed Bleda with his own hands. After having become the sole ruler of the Huns, Attila prepared for a large-scale invasion of Roman lands. Instead of first attacking the Western Empire, he decided to move again against the Eastern Empire by invading the Balkans. His violent raids ruined the economy of many Roman provinces, including Thrace, which were devastated again by the Huns. The Roman authorities in the east had no choice but to increase the annual tribute that they paid to the Huns. While operating in the Balkans, Attila established a secret channel of communication with Honoria, sister of Valentinian III and daughter of Galla Placidia. Honoria was a very ambitious woman who had already plotted against the other members of her family to secure the imperial throne. She sent a ring to Attila together with a request of help: in exchange for the Huns' military support, she would assign lands and privileges to Attila. After receiving Honoria's ring, Attila claimed her as his bride and half of the Western Empire as a dowry. It was the perfect *casus belli* for the Huns to launch their invasion.

In 451, the large-scale invasion of the Western Empire that Attila had long prepared for finally took place. By that time, Roman control over the vast region of Gaul that was the Huns' primary target was only nominal, the whole countryside being dominated by the Germanic communities that had invaded Gaul at the beginning of the fifth century AD. A significant Roman military presence could be found only in the major urban centres, while the *limes*, or frontier, of the Rhine River was almost defenceless. Northern Gaul was in the hands of the Franks, who were settled between the Rhine and the Lys River; the area crossed by the Garonne River was controlled by the Visigoths; the Burgundians were settled in south-western Gaul; and the Alans had established themselves along the Loire River. The Alans, as we will see in one of the next chapters, were a nomadic people of the steppes from Central Asia, and thus had a lot in common with the Huns. Differently from the other barbarian communities living in Gaul, they were extremely loyal to the Roman authorities. Flavius Aetius had the difficult task of controlling the various foreign communities living on the territory of Roman Gaul, but it was one that he performed with great intelligence. The Germanic *foederati*, or allies, living on imperial soil were extremely strong from a military point of view but were divided by deep internal rivalries, a situation that Flavius Aetius used to his advantage in order to avoid the formation of a large Germanic alliance that could threaten the very survival of the Western Empire. When the invasion of the Huns materialized, Flavius Aetius had no choice but to form a multi-ethnic alliance that comprised all the barbarian peoples living in

Gaul: the Franks, Visigoths, Burgundians and Alans. Having established their new homelands in Gaul, they were all keen to defend against the nomadic invaders. Nevertheless, it was not easy for Flavius Aetius to convince the various barbarian warlords to put aside their contrasting interests in order to face a common menace. Attila invaded the Western Empire with his own multi-ethnic army that had a lot in common with the forces of Flavius Aetius that were facing him. During the previous years, the Huns had submitted all the Germanic peoples living in Eastern Europe and transformed them into allies. All these Germanic communities were forced by Attila to participate in the invasion of Gaul by providing sizeable auxiliary contingents. These vassals of the Huns included the Ostrogoths, Rugians, Sciri, Thuringians, Gepids and Heruli. They were all extremely warlike and had ambitions of settling in the Western Empire. The Ostrogoths, or Eastern Goths, had been the fiercest enemies of the Visigoths, or Western Goths, for several decades. The Germanic warriors fighting as part of Flavius Aetius's alliance and those under Attila's orders fought in the same way, being equipped as infantry spearmen, although the Alans provided horse archers and armoured cavalrymen comparable to those of the Huns.

Attila crossed the Rhine in the early weeks of 451, probably at Strasbourg, before rapidly advancing by following the Roman roads. His large army, probably numbering around 100,000 men, attacked

Hun light cavalryman equipped with a spear and composite bow. (*Colour plate by Patricio Greve Moller, copyright by Gabriele Esposito*)

and destroyed several important urban settlements: Worms, Mainz, Trier, Metz and Reims. A large portion of northern Gaul was devastated by the invaders until they reached Aurelianum (modern Orleans) in the early summer of 451. Attila hoped to take the city swiftly, but met unexpectedly strong resistance. The inhabitants of Orleans, supported by the Alans, were able to repulse the Huns' attacks thanks to the strong walls of their city and resisted until the army of Flavius Aetius in Gaul was fully mobilized. Soon after the Huns crossed the Rhine, the Roman general had moved some military contingents from Italy to Gaul, after which he had talks with the powerful king of the Visigoths, Theodoric, in order to persuade him to join the anti-Hun alliance that was in the process of being formed. Initially, Theodoric was reluctant to fight with the Romans, preferring to wait for the arrival of the Huns in his domains. Eventually, however, the Visigoths also mobilized their troops and joined the other components of Flavius Aetius's army at Arles. On 14 June, after a relatively short march, the Romano-Germanic army reached the city of Orleans, where Attila, in order to avoid encirclement, had no choice but to abandon the siege and move back towards the Rhine. The leader of the Huns, keen to fight a decisive pitched battle against Flavius Aetius, wanted to choose a suitable battlefield on which he could display the superiority of his cavalry.

As a result, to gain some time, he left behind his Gepid allies with orders to slow down the advance of the enemy. Attila's rearguard was soon destroyed by the spearhead of Flavius Aetius, which was made up of Franks. Despite this, the Huns were able to reach a vast plain – known as the Catalaunian Fields – that was perfect for their combat tactics. The battlefield was extremely flat, rising only on one side with a sharp slope to a ridge that dominated the surrounding areas and quickly became the centre of the upcoming clash. Attila seized the right side of the ridge, while Flavius Aetius occupied the left, with the crest held by neither of the opposing forces. Attila deployed his elite Huns in the centre of his line, with the Ostrogoths on the left and the other Germanic auxiliaries on the right. The Huns faced the Alans, who occupied Flavius Aetius's centre; the Ostrogoths opposed the hated Visigoths, while the Germanic auxiliaries faced the Roman contingents. Attila initiated the battle by launching a devastating attack against his enemy's centre, but against all odds this was repulsed. The Huns invested Flavius Aetius's forces with a rain of arrows, but the shield wall formation of the Roman-Germanic soldiers resisted. The horse archers were repulsed with significant losses, which had a significant psychological impact on the Huns. Meanwhile, on the ridge, the Visigoths and the Ostrogoths fought with incredible violence. Many hundreds of Germanic warriors were killed in terrible hand-to-hand fighting, in which Theodoric was killed. Eventually, however, despite losing their king, the Visigoths prevailed and forced the Ostrogoths to fall

Hun horse archer. (*Colour plate by Patricio Greve Moller, copyright by Gabriele Esposito*)

back on the centre of Attila's line. This blocked any possibility of launching a fresh attack with the Hunnic horse archers and determined the outcome of the battle. The Visigoths assaulted the enemy centre with incredible fury, forcing Attila to seek refuge in his own camp, located in the rear of his army. The camp was fortified with wagons, as was usual way for the Germanic peoples, but the Visigoths – led by Theodoric's son, Thorismund – attacked it. Flavius Aetius, seeing that his enemies had suffered significant losses, ordered the Visigoths to suspend their assault and reorganized his line, which now controlled the ridge. When darkness came, it became apparent that the encounter had been won by the Romano-Germanic army. On the following day, Attila, whose supply lines were overstretched and whose allies no longer had the heart to fight, left the Catalaunian Fields with the remnants of his army and decided to suspend his invasion of Gaul.

The Battle of the Catalaunian Fields was a crucial turning point in the destiny of Western Europe, since it stopped a massive nomadic invasion and – for the first time – saw the Romans and the Germanic peoples sharing a common identity in order to face a mortal menace. The clash, however, did not signal the end for Attila and his Huns, who launched another invasion against the Western Empire during 452. This time the target was Italy, with Attila wanting to capture Ravenna and claim half of the imperial lands for himself. Flavius Aetius, who by now knew the tactics of the Huns extremely well, tried to block Attila's advance through the Julian Alps. Despite the Huns having never before crossed such a massive mountain range, the strategy of Flavius Aetius failed because he was surprised by the rapidity of his enemies. Aquileia, the most important and richest Roman urban centre in north-eastern Italy, was besieged and destroyed by the Huns, who pillaged some of Italy's most abundant agricultural areas. Thousands of refugees abandoned the countryside to escape death, some of them moving to an area on the coast at the head of the Adriatic and creating a settlement that later gave birth to the modern city of Venice. Valentinian III, fearing imminent capture by Attila, left the imperial court at Ravenna and went to Rome, where he hoped that Pope Leo I could protect him. By the middle of the fifth century, the pope was one of the most influential leaders of the Roman Empire, able to exert a very strong moral influence. Flavius Aetius, unlike what had happened in Gaul the previous year, could not count on significant military forces or strong Germanic allies. He remained quite passive during the campaign, simply trying to block the roads passing through the Apennines mountain range that connected Ravenna to Rome. Attila halted at the Po River to reorganize his forces and his overstretched supply lines. While camped on the banks of the Po, the Huns were visited by a Roman embassy that included Pope Leo I, who held talks with Attila and tried to convince him that by destroying Rome he would massacre thousands of innocent civilians. After the intervention of the pope, Attila decided to suspend his invasion of Italy and to return to Pannonia with the vast amounts of riches that he had pillaged.

Several ancient and medieval historians, writing about Attila's invasion of Italy from a religious perspective, attributed to Pope Leo I the success of having persuaded the king of the Huns to return back home. In reality, Attila was not convinced by the words of the pope, but by a number of practical features: his large army was suffering from lack of food and was being decimated by the diseases that were common along the banks of the Po. In addition, Attila had received news from Pannonia that his bases there were going to be attacked by Roman forces that had crossed the Danube. A new emperor, Marcian, was now on the throne of Constantinople, and he halted tribute payments to the Huns and prepared his forces for a confrontation with Attila. Since the Huns mostly funded their military campaigns with the gold received from the Eastern Empire, Attila had no option but to go back to Pannonia in order to prepare a new punitive invasion of the Balkans. Italy and the Western Empire were safe, at least for the moment. In 453, the two great protagonists of the Battle of the Catalaunian Fields died: Flavius Aetius was assassinated during a plot that was ordered by Valentinian III (who was himself killed soon after by soldiers who had remained loyal to Flavius Aetius), while Attila died of a haemorrhage on his wedding night. The fact that the king had died while celebrating his latest marriage made many contemporary historians suspect that Attila had been poisoned, probably by his new wife, Ildico, who had Ostrogoth origins. Some even suggested that the assassination had been organized in Constantinople, but there is no evidence to say that this was the case.

Following Attila's death, the immense empire that he had created at the head of the Huns very rapidly collapsed. A violent internal struggle for power saw the Huns fighting against their Germanic vassals, who revolted against their overlords in order to regain their freedom and conquer Pannonia for themselves. The Gepids, under the guidance of King Ardaric, formed a strong alliance that comprised the Heruli, Rugii, Sciri and Suebi. The Germanic coalition confronted the Huns at the Battle of Nedao, which took place in Pannonia near a tributary of the Sava River, in 454. The Huns, commanded by Ellak, the oldest son of Attila, were crushed by their opponents and Ellak was killed during the fighting. Following this setback, the Huns lost most of their prestige but remained a considerable power in Eastern Europe for some time. In 461, the second son of Attila, Dengizich, who had succeeded his older brother, was defeated by the Ostrogoths and had to face an internal rebellion led by his younger brother, Ernak. Together with his followers, Ernak seceded from the territories controlled by Dengizich, initiating a period of internal divisions for the Huns that led to their final decay. In 467, Dengizich attacked the Roman territories in the Balkans in the hope of restoring the Huns' former power, but had to face an unexpected offensive mounted by the Ostrogoths and his campaign failed completely. Dengizich was attacked by the Romans in Thrace, where he was defeated and killed in 469. Ernak tried to reunify the Huns after the death of his brother, but with limited success. Following Ernak's death, the Huns were divided into a series of small groups that were rapidly absorbed by the new nomadic peoples that came into Eastern Europe. The Bulgars, in particular, seem to have absorbed significant numbers of Huns, since Ernak – the last direct heir of Attila – is listed in some primary sources as the first leader of the Bulgars. As the events described above make clear, the leadership of Attila was the only thing capable of keeping together a people such as the Huns and controlling a vast empire stretching from Hungary in the west to the Caucasus in the east. The key element that determined the fall of the Huns' power in Eastern Europe was the revolt of the Germanic peoples who had previously been vassals of Attila, especially the Ostrogoths, who wanted to establish themselves within the Roman Empire and did not share the nomadic lifestyle of the Huns. Furthermore, they were extremely jealous of their freedom and did not want to be part of a larger political entity. The Huns' failures in their attempts to

Sarmatian warrior from the Hunnic era.
(*Photo by Tamás Ariel Horváth, alias Pharnakes the Sarmatian, copyright by Ádám Szuromi*)

conquer the Western Empire convinced their Germanic vassals they would be better off operating independently from the Huns against the Romans. A few decades later, this decision paid off when the former vassals of Attila settled on the territory of the Western Empire and caused its definitive fall. Nevertheless, it is important to remember that without the mass migration of the Huns, many Germanic peoples – such as the Goths – would have never moved towards the borders of the Roman Empire, so the military campaigns of Attila can be considered as one of the main factors behind the collapse of the Western Empire.

Not all the Huns living in Central Asia abandoned their homeland around AD 370 to migrate westwards, with a significant portion of the Hunnic communities preferring to remain in Asia. As a result, during the 370s, the Huns divided into two separate groups that had completely different destinies: the Black or Western Huns and the White or Eastern Huns. As we have seen, the Black Huns, under the guidance of Attila, invaded the Roman Empire after settling in Eastern Europe. The White Huns, meanwhile, also known as Hephthalites, were a significant power in Central Asia for a long time and had a longer history compared to that of the Black Huns. Around 450, the White Huns started to expand their territories by conquering the large region of Bactria, which connected Iran and Central Asia to the rich lands of northern India. The White Huns, thanks to their excellent combat skills, obtained a series of victories over the other nomadic peoples living around them and started nurturing an ambition of conquering India. They also clashed with the Sasanian Empire that controlled Iran, which strove to counter the expansionism of the nomads. Initially, the Sasanians obtained a series of victories over the White Huns, but the Huns gradually gained the upper hand and by 484 had taken some key frontier areas from the Sasanians. In 457, the Hephthalites sent an embassy to China and established positive relations with the Chinese authorities. The following year, they attacked the Sasanian Empire. By the beginning of the sixth century, thanks to their campaigns of conquest, the White Huns already controlled a vast empire that stretched from the deserts of Turkmenistan as far as the Caspian Sea, as well as the whole of Bactria and Sogdia. The Huns also occupied parts Afghanistan, making them a great potential threat to the political stability of northern India.

During the mid-sixth century, however, the strategic situation started to change, largely due to the military renaissance of the Sasanians under their great emperor, Khosrow I. Recognizing the White Huns as a significant rival power, Khosrow employed all his military resources in an attempt to destroy them. After expelling the Hephthalites from the regions bordering Iran, he conquered significant portions of present-day Pakistan and Afghanistan. To defeat the White Huns on the plains of Central Asia, Khosrow allied himself with the Turkic peoples, an emerging steppe power that had created – around 552 – a tribal state in Mongolia. In 557, at the Battle of Bukhara, a powerful alliance comprising Sasanian and Turkic forces defeated the Huns. The White Huns never recovered from this clash, their empire soon fragmenting into several semi-independent principalities that had little military power. These principalities were tributaries of the Sasanians or the Turkic peoples. The Sasanians and their allies established a frontier for their zones of influence in Central Asia along the Oxus River, with the White Huns' principalities functioning as buffer states between two large empires. After the death of Khosrow I in 579, the Hephthalites revolted against the Sasanians, but their rebellion was soon crushed by the Turkic peoples, who thus became the new overlords of the Huns living in Central Asia. In 588, having collaborated with the Sasanians for a lengthy period, their former Turkic allies invaded their lands by crossing the Oxus River. The White Huns joined with the Turkic forces and invaded a large part of the Sasanian territories, but were eventually repelled by their enemies. The decades following these events saw a progressive decay of the Sasanian Empire, which had to wage war on several fronts against multiple enemies (including the Eastern Romans and the rising power of the Arabs). This was taken advantage of by the White Huns, who began raiding the Sasanian Empire as far as Ispahan in central Iran. In 606, there was a further war between the Sasanians and the Turkic peoples, with the Huns participating on the Turkic side. The Hephthalites obtained several early victories before the Sasanians could mobilize their full military potential. Around 625, the eastern principalities of the White Huns finally lost what remained of their political freedom, being annexed by their ever-expanding former Turkic allies. The western principalities of the Hephthalites became involved in the campaigns fought between the Sasanians and the Arabs around 650. The Huns supported the Sasanians against the Muslim invaders, but their desperate resistance proved in vain: by 652, all the White Huns had been forced to pay tribute to the Arabs and accept Muslim garrisons on their territories. The independent history of the Hephthalites was over.

The economy of the Huns was not based on agriculture but on various kinds of domesticated animals. They herded sheep and goats for milk, meat, wool and skins, as well as cattle for milk, meat and hides. They also had many horses, which played a vital role in controlling such large herds over the huge distances of the steppes. The Huns, being nomadic herdsmen, moved with their extended families across the vast plains of their home territories in order to seek the best opportunities for grazing and trading as the seasons changed. The extended families were grouped into clans, whose numerical consistency usually fluctuated greatly since families could move from one group to another according to circumstances. Quite often, the number of families making up a clan increased during the summer and decreased during

Hun warrior armed with a sword. (*Photo by Dimitar Atanasov, IEFSEM-BAS, Experiencing History Research Project, copyright by Jordan Sivkov – Leather Works, Dobrich, Bulgaria*)

the winter, depending on the availability of pasture. Each clan or group worked as a herding camp and had its own hereditary pastures. Driving their grazing herds before them, the Huns trundled onwards with their families and all their goods. They lived in black tents made of felt that were packed in wagons. They followed set migratory routes and used traditional camping grounds. In general, however, their life was tough and precarious. A young Hun learned how to endure cold, hunger and thirst from his early years. The Hunnic lifestyle was also characterized by continuous skirmishes with other nomadic peoples that took place in the steppes. Plundering expeditions were extremely common, aimed at stealing animals from the camps of rival groups. Large cavalry battles could also be fought for the conquest of camping grounds, control of which could determine the survival of an entire clan. Hun boys were taught from an early age to ride horses with and without saddles, as well as to use the deadly composite bow of the steppes with great precision. The Huns were excellent hunters, and their composite bows were also used for hunting. Indeed, by grouping their herds and hunting in the steppe plains, they practiced the same movements and actions on which their battle tactics were based. From an economic point of view, the Huns were almost self-sufficient, although they had to obtain some amounts of grain through barter or as a tribute from the sedentary peoples whom they had submitted. The composite bow represented the greatest empowerment for a Hun individual over the environment in which he lived. A young Hun, for example, had to master the use of the horse and the composite bow in order to persuade the elders of his clan that he might – in time – become an effective horse archer. All the able-bodied male individuals of the Hunnic society were warriors, and many women also knew how to fight. In time of war, however, the women's primary duty was to protect the herds and tents of the clan from enemy attacks.

The wild appearance of the Huns made them look terrifying to contemporary Roman observers, who had never before been in contact with a people from the steppes of Central Asia. The Huns usually wore their hair cut back to the temples – leaving the hair behind to hang untidily to a great length – and shaved their cheeks. These were often ceremonially scarred with deep wounds, which were considered to be warrior adornments. The Huns also practiced cranial deformation, in order to have elongated skulls in a fashion that was common to several steppe peoples. Cranial deformation was carried out by binding in early childhood, when the skull is still soft and growing. Apparently, however, only a limited number of individuals had a deformed skull, as this distinguished members of the ruling families that made up the elite of the Hunnic society. Ceremonial scars, though, were typical of all the warriors who had some combat experience. The basic dress of the Huns was extremely simple, consisting of a short-sleeved tunic made of natural wool or goat hair, which was worn to the knee and slit to the waist, where it was gathered by a belt. Breeches were worn loose and tied around the ankles. Tall leather boots were in general use, being made of ox-hide and having heelless soles made from soft leather. Felt stockings could be worn inside the boots during cold months. The winters also saw the use of furred kaftans, which had extra-long sleeves that were designed to act as hand warmers. One breast of the kaftan crossed over the other and was tied to one side. During winter, two kaftans could be worn at the same time, one with the hair turned outwards and the other with it turned inwards. The standard headgear of the Huns was a goatskin cap with earflaps or a felt hat trimmed with fox skin. The type of fur used to produce the clothes of an individual indicated their social rank: commoners wore the fur of dogs and wolves, while noblemen were clad in the fur of sables or squirrels. Hunnic garments were sewn together using a tough thread made of twisted sinew.

According to the ancient sources available, the armies of the Huns comprised a high percentage of mounted archers and only a limited number of armoured cavalrymen. The infantry were provided entirely by the Germanic peoples who were vassals of the Huns. The Hunnic mounted archer, equipped with a composite bow, did not wear a helmet or armour. Although he could sometimes carry a light spear and a sword, he was not used to fighting at

Hun mercenary in Roman service; the embroidering of the tunic shows a clear Late Roman influence. (*Colour plate by Patricio Greve Moller, copyright by Gabriele Esposito*)

close range. The Hunnic light spears were used both for thrusting and throwing, but were of little use against an enemy equipped with a shield or cuirass. The Hunnic swords were made of iron and were of a long-hilted type. Also long-bladed and double-edged, the swords had been copied by the Huns from the Sasanians. The Hunnic swords were designed for cutting and for mounted use, but their quality was quite poor because the Huns – differently from the Scythians and Sarmatians – did not produce durable metal weapons. The Black Huns, unlike the White Huns, also carried a dagger that hung horizontally across the belly; this was used quite rarely, only when a warrior was forced to fight hand-to-hand. The personal equipment of a mounted archer was simple but very effective: it included a bow-case that was carried on the front of the left thigh and a quiver that was hung either from a belt or across the small of the back, with the points of the arrows to the right. A small circular shield of willow, wood or hide could be carried, strapped to the left forearm, its main function being to protect the bowman from enemy arrows. It was designed for the duels that took place on the Eurasian steppes between horse archers, who fired at each other from distance. The few armoured cavalrymen were aristocrat warriors and members of the elite of the Hunnic society. Their body armour had lamellar construction and reached to the waist or the knee. Only the chieftains and their personal retinues had cuirasses, which consisted of narrow vertical plates laced together horizontally and vertically. The lamellar armour worn by the Huns was constructed according to the practices of Central Asia. The Hunnic helmets were of the spangenhelm type and had many features in common with those used by the Sarmatians. They were constructed from several plates, usually six, held together in conical form by reinforcing bands. In their basic form, they looked like a sort of skullcap, but some of the richest warriors could add extra elements to them such as cheek-pieces, neck-guards and nasal-guards.

Compared with the Scythians and the Sarmatians, the Huns did not deploy significant contingents of shock heavy cavalry; indeed, they are not mentioned in any Roman source. Apparently, however, the heavy cavalry of the White Huns was more numerous than those of the Black Huns. The fact that the Hunnic heavy cavalry did not employ the *kontus* spear implies that their mounted troops did not consist of cataphracts. Furthermore, due to their limited numbers, they probably did not play a significant tactical role on the battlefield. The same could be said of the infantry, which the Black Huns started to have only after settling in Eastern Europe. Consisting of foreign warriors, they performed only auxiliary duties and were taken into little consideration by the Hun military commanders. Over time, however, Attila had to accept the fact that some effective infantry were needed if he wanted to invade the Roman Empire: only foot troops could operate during sieges and

Germanic auxiliary infantryman in Hunnic service. (*Photo by Ádám Baumgartner, alias Isenbrand the Skirii, copyright by Zoltán Krasznay*)

perform hand-to-hand fighting against the Roman heavy infantry. During Attila's failed invasions of the Western Empire, as we have seen, the Hunnic infantry were mostly provided by the Germanic vassals, who sometimes performed very well (as the Ostrogoths did at the Battle of the Catalaunian Fields). The loyalty of the Germanic auxiliaries, however, could not be counted upon, as the events following Attila's death clearly showed. The amazing power of the Hunnic horse archers was the result of two factors: their composite bows and their horses. The horses ridden by the Huns were tough and rough-coated; they had short legs and were just 12–14 hands high. Their smallness and muscular nature allowed the Huns to wield considerable control over them and provided a suitable platform for mounted archery. Many of the Hunnic stallions were gelded to make them easier to handle, according to a custom that had ancient origins. The animals used by the Hun warriors were branded with the emblem of their owner's clan or by cutting a pattern on their ears.

The horse breeds living on the steppes could be fed on virtually any quality of pasturage, as they were capable of fending for themselves in the severe conditions of their natural environment. The ability of their mounts to cope well with hard riding and easily gain sustenance gave a decisive advantage to the mounted warriors of the Huns during the extended raids that they conducted. Their steeds did not require the carting of fodder but were simply let loose at the end of a day's riding to fend

Heavy cavalryman of the White Huns armed with a mace. Both the clothes and the equipment show a certain Sasanian influence. (*Colour plate by Patricio Greve Moller, copyright by Gabriele Esposito*)

Horse archer of the White Huns.
(*Photo by Csongrádi Turán HSE, copyright by Hungarian Turan Foundation, Tamás Horváth*)

for themselves. The ugly appearance of the Hunnic horses was compensated by their resilience, which impressed contemporary Roman observers. The Hunnic horses were far better at climbing, jumping and swimming than the Roman mounts. As they were used to living in a semi-wild manner, they could endure almost any hardship.

Hun horse archer. (*Photo by Attila Kiss and Tömör, copyright by Kőmíves Nelli Admira*)

Sarmatian flask and ring-pommel short sword from the Hunnic era.
(*Photo by Tamás Ariel Horváth, alias Pharnakes the Sarmatian, copyright by Ádám Szuromi*)

During cold months, when their mounts were weaker due to the climatic conditions, the Huns travelled with a number of reserve horses to ensure that they always had a fresh mount when needed. The Huns were capable of riding without interruption for an entire day, and could thus travel enormous distances in a relatively short period of time. The riding equipment of the Huns was quite rudimentary since – according to the latest research – they did not use stirrups, exactly like the Scythians and the Sarmatians. Neither did they use spurs, but urged their horses on with riding whips. The Hunnic saddle was known as a frame saddle and was quite comfortable to use. It consisted of a wooden frame with leather cushioning on either side. The version employed by the Black Huns also had a straight vertical arch in front and a larger arch behind.

Hunnic battle tactics, like those of all the steppe peoples, derived from herd management. The Huns usually approached the enemy in a loose crescent formation, which threatened less mobile opponents with encirclement around their flanks. If resisted at any point, the Huns would stage a feigned retreat to draw the enemy out of their chosen position and into a dangerous pursuit. The Huns were masters at firing arrows what was known as the 'Parthian shot' – turning their bodies while riding away from their enemy to shoot at any pursuers – as well as in organizing deadly ambushes. As already mentioned, they avoided engaging in close combat and usually won battles with their volleys of arrows shot at long range. Striking fast and hard was the main characteristic of Hunnic warfare, the sudden incursions of the Huns being so rapid that sedentary peoples – such as the Romans – were incapable of effectively countering them. The ability to shoot arrows with extraordinary accuracy and power while at full gallop made the Hunnic horse archers more than a match for any kind of enemy cavalry. Being fast and unpredictable, the Hunnic cavalry could route any major mounted force deployed on the field by the Romans. However, the same could not be said for their Germanic infantry, since the Huns always experienced significant tactical difficulties when facing contingents of heavy infantrymen deployed in a shield wall defensive formation. This happened, for example, during the Battle of the Catalaunian Fields, which proved decisive in the failure of Attila's invasion of Gaul. When the Huns lost their political control over some of the Germanic peoples, they also lost the possibility to conquer the Roman Empire since they were not capable – alone – of confronting large infantry armies or conducting siege operations.

Chapter 3

The Avars, 557–830

Following the collapse of the Hunnic Empire created by Attila and the fall of the Western Roman Empire, Eastern Europe entered a period of great turmoil, characterized by the migrations of several different peoples. Many of the Germanic communities that had been vassals of the Huns, like the Ostrogoths, entered the territories of the former Western Empire and established their own Romano-Germanic kingdoms in Europe, which created a power vacuum in some strategic areas of Eastern Europe such as Pannonia. At the same time, the progressive decay of the White Huns in Asia favoured the rapid ascendancy of the Turkic peoples, who created an immense empire of the steppes that extended itself from Manchuria in the east to the Caucasus in the west. The formation of this Turkic state, commonly known as the First Turkic Khaganate, led to the beginning of a series of migrations, several steppe groups preferring to abandon their homelands rather than be submitted by the ascendant Turkic peoples. This was the case with the Avars, a nomadic people of the steppes of whose origins we know very little. According to the most recent studies, the Avars originated somewhere on the territory of Mongolia and Manchuria, probably in the same years that saw the great campaigns of the Huns in Europe. In the mid-sixth century, coming under severe military pressure from the First Turkic Khaganate, they began moving westwards with the intention of settling on the Pontic Steppe of Ukraine. The Avars officially appeared on the political scene of Eastern Europe in 557, when they sent an embassy to Constantinople after having already settled in the northern Caucasus. In exchange for some payments in gold, they agreed to pacify the Caucasus on behalf of the Eastern Romans – who could now be called Byzantines, since the Western Roman Empire was no longer in existence. At that time, the Byzantine Empire was ruled by Emperor Justinian, probably the greatest monarch in the history of the Eastern Empire. Justinian had ambitions to reconquer most of the Roman western provinces that had been occupied by the Germanic peoples during the previous decades, and thus his attention was mostly focused on Western Europe. He had no interest in fighting costly wars for the control of a marginal frontier area like the Caucasus, and consequently accepted coming to terms with the newly arrived Avars. Having been extremely successful in pacifying the Caucasus, the Avars soon started to expand across the steppes north

Magyar chieftain wearing lamellar cuirass.
(*Photo by Vermes Tribe, copyright by Hungarian Turan Foundation, Tamás Horváth*)

Avar standard-bearer.
(*Photo by Anda Lovasharc SE, copyright by Hungarian Turan Foundation, Tamás Horváth*)

Magyar standard-bearer.

(Photo by Magyar Turán HSE, copyright by Hungarian Turan Foundation, Tamás Horváth)

of the Black Sea. They reached the basin of the lower Danube and appeared on the northern borders of the Balkans.

By 562, the Avars were determined to conquer rich pastoral lands south of the Danube, and could achieve their objective by either negotiating with the Byzantines or fighting against them. Before attacking the Byzantine Empire, however, the Avars concentrated their efforts on occupying the large plains of the Carpathian Basin. Comprising the whole territory of present-day Hungary, this region had always been the homeland of the nomadic peoples of the steppes migrating towards Eastern Europe. Apart from the steppes in Ukraine, the Hungarian plains were the only area of Eastern Europe where a nomadic people could find the pastures needed to feed many thousands of horses. Due to its geographical position, the Carpathian Basin was also perfect to act as a military base from which to launch incursions against both Germany and Italy in the west and the Balkans in the east. When the Avars arrived in Eastern Europe, the Carpathian Basin was controlled by the Gepids. This Germanic people had played a prominent role in determining the fall of the Hunnic Empire and had thereby become a significant regional power in Eastern Europe after the defeat of the Huns. The Gepids had become allies of the Byzantine Empire and had slowly started to exert their influence over the other Germanic communities living in or around Pannonia. During the central part of the sixth century, however, a new Germanic people from Scandinavia migrated to the Carpathian Basin and entered the territory of Pannonia: the Lombards. These were an extremely warlike and wild people, according to contemporary observers, having experienced very little contact with Roman civilization during the previous centuries and being the last Germanic people to migrate. Soon after their arrival in Pannonia, fighting broke out between the Lombards and the Gepids.

The Avars, after seeing that the Lombards were causing serious military problems for the Gepids, entered the inter-Germanic conflict on the side of the Lombards. Within a few months, by joining their forces, the Avars and the Lombards destroyed the powerful realm of the Gepids and occupied the whole of Pannonia. However, it soon became apparent that the Avars and the Lombards could not live together on the same territory, the Avars being much stronger than their new allies. The Lombards, realizing that a war with the Avars would cause their complete destruction, preferred maintaining positive relations with them and thus decided to migrate westwards into Italy. There, from 568 onwards, they obtained a series of brilliant victories over the Byzantines and were thereby able to establish their own independent kingdom that controlled most of the Italian peninsula. The Lombard invasion of Italy, caused by the expansionism of the Avars, was the last Germanic mass movement of the so-called Migration Period. After conquering Pannonia, the

Magyar standard-bearer.
(*Photo by Anda Lovasharc SE, copyright by Hungarian Turan Foundation, Tamás Horváth*)

Magyar heavy cavalryman equipped with a full set of lamellar armour.
(*Photo by Magyar Turán HSE, copyright by Hungarian Turan Foundation, Tamás Horváth*)

Avars became one of the major military powers of Eastern Europe and a serious menace to the survival of the Byzantine Empire. The Byzantines, knowing very well that a confrontation with the Avars was imminent, tried to gain time by inviting them to occupy the border areas located around the mouth of the Danube. This, however, was not enough for the Avars, who – in just a few years – created a large state in the Carpathian Basin that became known as the Avar Khaganate. This

Avar heavy cavalryman wearing lamellar helmet.
(*Photo by Anda Lovasharc SE, copyright by Hungarian Turan Foundation, Tamás Horváth*)

region was inhabited not only by the Avars, but also by the Germanic and Slavic tribes that the nomads had progressively transformed into their vassals. In 579, the Byzantine Emperor Tiberius II decided to suspend the payment of tributes that his state sent to the Avars, which provoked the Avars to invade the Balkans and marked the beginning of the Byzantine-Avar Wars.

In 581, after several months of campaigning, the Avars conquered the major city of Sirmium, which was one of the Byzantines' main military bases in the northern Balkans. They then began pillaging a large portion of the Balkans, obtaining a series of spectacular victories. At that time, the Byzantines were also fighting a major war in the Middle East against the Sasanian Empire, meaning their garrisons on the Danube frontier were undermanned and underpaid. Consequently, the Avars could raid most of the Balkans without encountering any serious resistance. They were followed by substantial numbers of Slavs, who took advantage of the Avar invasion to enter the borders of the Byzantine Empire in great numbers. For ten years, until 591, the Avars and their Slavic subjects spread terror and violence across the very heartland of the Byzantine Empire. This had significant economic consequences for the Byzantines and almost caused the collapse of their state. In 591, Emperor Maurice, an experienced military commander, signed a ceasefire treaty with the Sasanian Empire in order to shift his military resources to the Balkans. The veteran Byzantine military forces coming from the Middle East routed several raiding parties of the Avars and then crossed the Danube to attack the Slavs in their new settlements. By 594, the Byzantine troops had established a solid presence on the Danube frontier, which halted the organization of new pillaging campaigns by the Avars. During 595 and 596, the Avars ceased their attacks against the Byzantine Empire to reorganize themselves for a major new offensive. In 597, a large Byzantine army was destroyed by the Avars, who thereafter rapidly advanced towards Constantinople. Once at the gates of Constantinople, however, they understood that they did not have the necessary resources to besiege such a large city for any length of time. Emperor Maurice offered them the payment of a large sum of money in exchange for a temporary truce, and this they accepted. Some months later, a formal peace treaty was signed and the Avars returned to their homeland. Constantinople was safe, but it was clear to Emperor Maurice that the nomads would soon return. In 599, the Byzantines mounted a major counter-offensive against the Avars, crossing the Danube with the objective of invading the Avar Khaganate. Unexpectedly, the Byzantine offensive was successful, the Avars being defeated on the open field at the consecutive battles of Viminacium and being unable to prevent the devastation of large swathes of their lands. By 602, the Byzantines had regained full control over the course of the Danube and once again started to operate a fleet on the great river's course.

After decades of foreign incursions, Emperor Maurice had been able to restore order on the northern frontier of his state. He planned to repopulate the devastated lands that he had recovered by settling large Armenian communities on them, and intended organizing a new campaign with the objective of destroying the Avar Khaganate once and for all. In 602, however, Maurice was overthrown, leading to the outbreak of a chaotic political phase in the Byzantine Empire, a development that favoured the military recovery of the Avars. In 615, the new Emperor Heraclius withdrew most of the Byzantine troops stationed in the Balkans in order to face a new Sasanian offensive in the Middle East. This encouraged the Avars and the Slavs to launch fresh incursions against the weakened Byzantine territories, with devastating consequences. By 626, the Byzantine Empire was again on the verge of collapse, with the Avars moving freely across the Balkans and the Sasanians in control of most of the Middle East. In order to destroy their common enemy, the Avars and Sasanians decided to cooperate, with the objective of conquering Constantinople. The Avars were to attack the Byzantine capital from the west, while the Sasanians moved against it from the east. The plan could have worked well, splitting the Byzantine forces with concurrent offensives, but it needed a high level of coordination to succeed. However, this was not easy to achieve, since the Byzantine fleet – the best in Europe and the Middle East at that moment – controlled the Bosporus and made communication between the two allies very difficult. Notwithstanding this problem, the Avars and the Slavs – roughly 80,000 men – launched a coordinated assault upon the walls of Constantinople on 29 June 626. This was repulsed, partly due to the lack of significant support from the Sasanians, who had their main naval base at Chalcedon (near Constantinople, on the Anatolian coastline). The Avar attacks continued without success for several weeks, until news of a defeat for the Sasanians in Anatolia reached Constantinople. Now having no naval forces at their disposal, and having already suffered significant losses, the Avars suspended the siege of the Byzantine capital and returned north.

The years following the failed siege of 626 were difficult ones for the Avars, who faced a series of massive revolts launched by their Slavic subjects. The Slavs, under the guidance of a capable politico-military leader named Samo, created a first form of unified Slavic polity that worked as a tribal confederacy. Guided by the Slavic Wends, the confederacy slowly freed itself from the rule of the Avar Khaganate and assumed control over large parts of their homeland. Samo was able to create a solid state, which controlled a portion of modern Poland as well as the present-day Czech Republic and Slovakia. By the end of his reign, the Slavs living in the northern area of Croatia had also freed themselves from Avar rule. At the same time, another steppe people arriving from Asia, the Bulgars, started to challenge the Avars' dominance over the

Magyar heavy cavalryman wearing a helmet with an attached piece of chainmail. (*Photo by Magyar Turán HSE, copyright by Hungarian Turan Foundation, Tamás Horváth*)

Avar heavy cavalryman equipped with a corselet of lamellar armour.
(*Photo by Anda Lovasharc SE, copyright by Hungarian Turan Foundation, Tamás Horváth*)

Magyar heavy cavalryman armed with spear and composite bow. (*Photo by Vermes Tribe, copyright by Hungarian Turan Foundation, Tamás Horváth*)

plains of Ukraine. Within a few years, the Bulgars were able to establish their own autonomous realm north of the Black Sea, which soon became extremely powerful. Having lost significant territories to the Slavs and the Bulgars, the Avar Khaganate was shattered by a series of civil wars and ran the risk of disappearing. After several difficult decades, however, the situation started to improve for the Avars, as both the Slavs and the Bulgars were weakened by internal struggles. Following Samo's death, in 658, some Slavic tribes returned under Avar rule after the disintegration of the tribal confederation overseen by the Wends. As for the Bulgars, their state in the Pontic Steppe began disintegrating from 665 and was progressively divided into five minor political entities that had contrasting interests. These events favoured a renaissance of Avar power in the Carpathian Basin, which duly took place during the closing decades of the seventh century. The Avar Khaganate gradually reconquered several of the territories that it had lost and reacquired its status as a regional power that it had enjoyed before the failed siege of Constantinople. During the first half of the eighth century, the Avars established very close diplomatic relations with the Lombard Kingdom of Italy, largely because the Avars and the Lombards now had a common enemy that was exerting increasing pressure on their borders: the Franks. Ruled by the emerging Carolingian family, the Franks were in the process of transforming their realm into the most powerful state of Europe.

The Franks, under the leadership of warlords such as the Carolingian Charles Martel, formed a strong political alliance with the papacy of Rome and started to extend their influence over a large area of Central Europe. Their ultimate ambition was to seize Italy from the Lombards, and in this they were supported by the Church of Rome, which had long wanted to eliminate the Lombard presence in the Italian peninsula because it feared that the Lombards might one day invade the lands of the papacy in central Italy. In 773, Charlemagne, the greatest of all the Carolingian monarchs, invaded the Lombard Kingdom, crossing the Alps at the head of a large army. After several months of harsh campaigning in northern Italy, the Franks prevailed and Charlemagne conquered the whole Lombard Kingdom. These events shocked the Avars, whose only reliable ally in Europe had been the Lombards. The Avar Khaganate now bordered with Frankish lands along its entire western frontier, since the Carolingians dominated most of Germany in addition to northern Italy. Until 780, Bavaria, albeit ruled by a Frankish noble family, remained independent from direct Carolingian rule. After Charlemagne also occupied Bavarian territory, however, it became apparent to the Avars that they had to react in some way to the Carolingians' expansionism. Indeed, Bavaria bordered with the heartland of the Avar Khaganate. Initially, the Avars tried to establish positive diplomatic relations with Charlemagne, but he showed no interest in making a peace treaty with them. As a result, during the 780s, the Avars started to provide assistance to several Lombard and Bavarian aristocrats who had left their nations as exiles due to the Carolingian invasions. This was perceived as a provocation by Charlemagne, who was struggling to achieve Bavaria's full integration into his vast realm. In 788, hostilities erupted between the Franks and the Avars, with a massive Avar incursion directed against both northern Italy and Bavaria. The two cavalry armies assembled by the nomads, however, were easily defeated by the Franks. In retaliation for the attacks, the Carolingians mounted a punitive expedition that crossed the eastern border of Bavaria before crushing the Avars on the Ybbs River. The Avar Khaganate responded by organizing a new and larger invasion of Bavaria, but this too was defeated by the Franks.

In the summer of 791, Charlemagne assembled a large army at Regensburg with the intention of invading the Avar Khaganate. The Avars now represented the most dangerous potential threat to the stability of the Frankish domains in Central Europe, and thus had to be destroyed. Charlemagne began the invasion by sending an elite cavalry force into the Avar Khaganate. These chosen heavy cavalrymen routed the enemy forces they encountered along the way and seized much booty before returning to the Frankish lands. This successful incursion was followed by a full Frankish offensive, which was conducted by two separate armies. They invaded the Avar Khaganate by marching along both banks of the Danube, supported by a newly built fleet that was tasked with supplying the Frankish troops. Charlemagne's invasion was successful in its first phase, with the Carolingian troops capturing all the Avar fortresses they encountered without facing any significant resistance from the enemy. At this point, however, pestilence broke out in the Frankish camp, with especially devastating effects on their horses. Around 90 per cent of the Carolingian horses died, which obliged Charlemagne to suspend his invasion and return to Bavaria. In 793, the Franks again penetrated the Avar Khaganate with some token cavalry forces, which successfully raided the Avar lands. Shortly after these events, a civil war broke out among the Avars, which was probably orchestrated by the Franks. This conflict ended with the ascendancy of a pro-Frankish Avar leader, who offered his subjugation to Charlemagne in exchange for the great king's protection. In 796, the Franks, together with their Slavic allies, attacked the Avar Khaganate once more, and even sacked the residence of the Avars' leader, or khagan. Located on the plains between the rivers Danube and Tisza, this was known as the 'ring' since it consisted of a palace settlement laid out in a circle that comprised both tents and wooden structures. The Franks sacked the 'ring' and seized much of its impressive treasures as booty. Following this astounding victory, the Franks invaded the Avar Khaganate again by following the same path used by Charlemagne in 791. This time, however,

Avar heavy cavalryman equipped with lamellar helmet.
(*Photo by Anda Lovasharc SE, copyright by Hungarian Turan Foundation, Tamás Horváth*)

Magyar heavy cavalryman.
(*Photo by Vermes Tribe,
copyright by Hungarian
Turan Foundation, Tamás
Horváth*)

Magyar heavy cavalryman equipped with a full set of lamellar armour.
(*Photo by Magyar Turán HSE, copyright by Hungarian Turan Foundation, Tamás Horváth*)

the Avars opted to surrender without a fight due to the great military superiority of their enemy. All the western territories of the Avar Khaganate were absorbed into the Frankish domains and many Avars were forced to become Christians by their conquerors. The eastern portion of the Avar lands was instead occupied by the Bulgars, who had established a powerful new state in the Balkans during the previous decades. By 830, the Avars had practically disappeared from history.

From a military point of view, the Avars underwent a significant evolution after settling in the Carpathian Basin, which eventually made them quite different from the other nomadic peoples. Following their failed siege of Constantinople, the Avars gradually became a semi-nomadic population, establishing some permanent settlements in their Pannonian homeland. By the time of the Carolingian invasions, the Avar Khaganate not only had a sort of capital (the famous 'ring') but also many fortified settlements that were inhabited on a permanent basis. Such settlements were modelled on the royal one of the 'ring', acting as citadels from which the Avars could control their territorial possessions. From a tactical point of view, the Avar armies were quite different from those of the Huns. They comprised large cavalry forces made up of heavy cavalrymen equipped with full armour, who were supported by significant numbers of horse archers. The excellence of the Avar heavy cavalry was due to the use of the stirrup, which was introduced into Europe from Central Asia by the Avars. Their cavalry tactics were based on devastating charges conducted by fully armoured horsemen, who could strike with their spears with a great deal of precision thanks to the riders' stability provided by the use of stirrups. The horse archers of the Avar armies were efficient and well-equipped, but played just a secondary role on the battlefield since their composite bows were used only to support the charges of the heavy cavalry. As was the case with the Huns, the elite mounted contingents of the Avars were supported by the auxiliary infantry provided by the communities that had been submitted by the Avar Khaganate. These were mostly Slavic ones, whose members all fought as light infantry and were equipped as spearmen or javelineers. Only the noble warriors of the Slavic tribes wore some form of armour, and none of the Slavic warriors fought on horseback. The Slavs also deployed some significant contingents of archers, but these were equipped with the longbow that was typical of Central Europe and not with the composite bow of the steppes. The society of the Avars was characterized by the presence of a small aristocracy, the members of which were all warriors and could equip themselves with impressive armour. Such nobles dominated the rest of the population and their Slavic subjects; the latter, at least during the first centuries of the Avar presence in Pannonia, lived separately from the Avars. However, the Slavs were progressively included in the Avars' state and became a very important component of Avar society. By the time of the Carolingian

Avar armoured horse archer. (*Photo by Attila Kiss and Tömör, copyright by Kőmíves Nelli Admira*)

invasions, the Avar Khaganate was inhabited by an elite of Avar nobles and a large number of common Slavic people.

The military equipment of the Avar heavy cavalry was quite peculiar, since they were armed not only with a spear but also with a composite bow. This enabled the Avar heavy horsemen to also operate – if needed – as mounted archers, not only as shock cavalry. Most of the Avar heavy horsemen wore lamellar cuirasses made of iron, but an alternative form of armour of heavy felt was also quite popular. The Avar nobles protected their horses with pieces of lamellar or felt armour, which covered the animals' heads and forequarters. A particular component of the Avars' heavy armour was a form of neck-protecting gorget, which they brought from Central Asia to Europe, like the horse armour described above. The Avar heavy cavalrymen employed extra-long spears of the *kontus* type, as well as shorter ones; both models of spear, however, were used for thrusting. The Avar composite bow was more curved and shorter than that used by the Huns, but it was extremely effective if employed from a medium distance. Avar swords were single-edged and had a straight blade, being designed not for cavalry combat but to be used against enemy foot troops

Magyar armoured horse archer.
(*Photo by Magyar Turán HSE, copyright by Hungarian Turan Foundation, Tamás Horváth*)

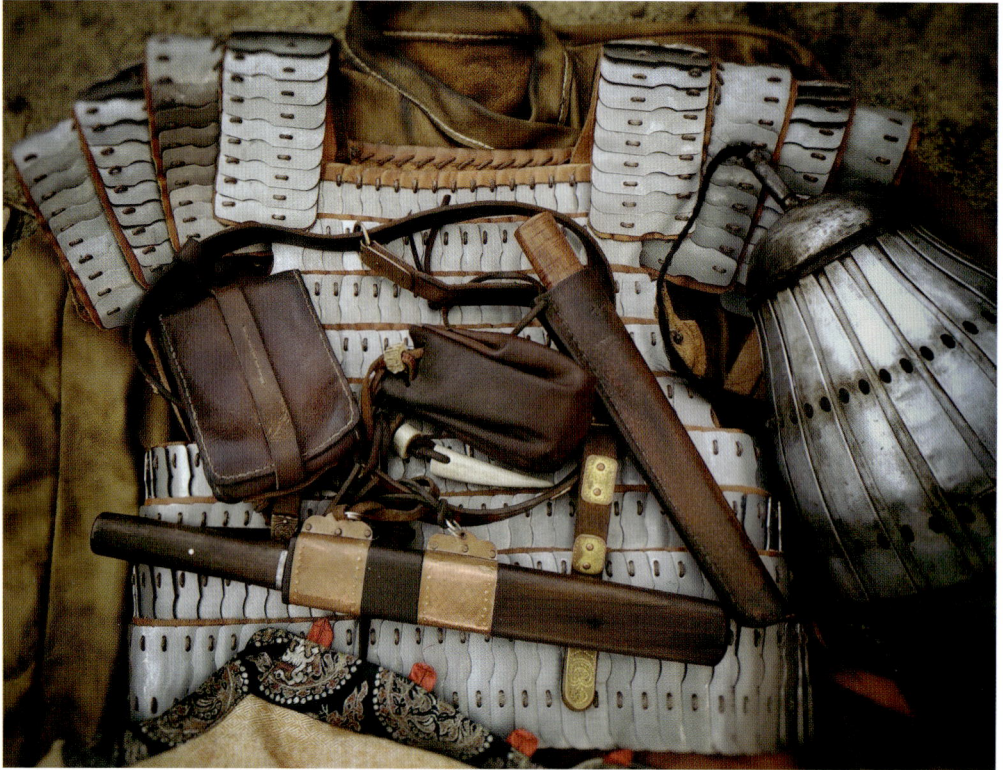

Corselet of lamellar armour, lamellar helmet and knives of an Avar warrior.
(*Photo by Ákos Kollár, copyright by Ákos Kollár*)

during frontal charges. The Avars – at least initially – wore long pigtails according to their traditional fashions, which gave them a quite different appearance than all the sedentary peoples living around them. Their loose-fitting tunics were designed for riding and were extremely comfortable to wear. The tunics could have rich decoration and embroidering if they belonged to nobles, and in some cases were even made of silk. The wood-framed saddles of the Avar cavalry, being an improved version of the Hunnic saddles, were extremely effective and were consequently copied by the Byzantines, who also adopted stirrups after campaigning against the Avars.

Detail showing the helmet and cuirass of a Magyar warrior.
(*Photo by Magyar Turán HSE, copyright by Hungarian Turan Foundation, Tamás Horváth*)

Avar warrior equipped with lamellar helmet and corselet of chainmail. (*Photo and copyright by Jan Kudělka*)

Avar warrior equipped with a full set of chainmail. (*Photo and copyright by Jan Kudělka*)

Slavic light infantryman equipped with helmet and shield.
(*Photo by Michal Pavlišta, copyright by Tereza Machačová*)

Slavic light infantryman armed with short axe.
(*Photo by Michal Pavlišta, copyright by Tereza Machačová*)

Chapter 4

The Magyars, 850–1000

Louis the Pious, the son and successor of Charlemagne, died on 20 June 840. This marked the end of the Carolingian Empire's unity, a major civil war breaking out soon after in Frankish territories between the three sons of the monarch (Lothair, Louis the German and Charles the Bald). In 842, Louis the German and Charles the Bald secured an alliance and declared Lothair unfit to rule with the Oaths of Strasbourg. These were an extremely important political act, but also of great cultural importance because Louis the German swore his oath in Romance (an early form of French) so that the soldiers of Charles the Bald could understand him, while Charles the Bald swore his oath in Germanic, enabling the troops of Louis the German to understand him. For the first time, some early forms of the future French and German languages had been used on an official occasion. In 843, the civil war came to an end with the signing of the Treaty of Verdun, which divided the Frankish Empire between the three sons. Lothair retained the imperial title, but was assigned a narrow strip of land located in the centre of the Frankish territories that extended from Frisia in the north to Provence in the south; he also received the Frankish lands in Italy. Louis the German was assigned all the Carolingian territories located east of the Rhine (Saxony, Alamannia and Bavaria), while Charles the Bald was to rule most of Gaul. Louis the German thus received the territories that later evolved to become Germany, while Charles the Bald was assigned the territories that eventually became France. The new realm of Lothair, due to its geographical features, was almost impossible to defend, making it militarily weak. In 855, following Lothair's death, the lands that had made up his realm were divided between his three sons: Louis inherited Italy and the imperial title, Lothair II received present-day Lorraine (an area that started to be known as Lotharingia) and Charles obtained Burgundy. In 858, the dissatisfied Louis allied himself with his uncle, Louis the German, against his brother, Lothair II, and the latter's ally, Charles the Bald. A further civil war fought between Carolingians thus began, which ended in 862 with no clear victor. One year later, Charles of Burgundy died without direct heirs and his realm was inherited by his brother, Louis. In 869, Lothair II also died without a direct successor, his kingdom being divided between Charles the Bald and Louis the German with the Treaty of Meerssen. Louis, the only surviving son

Magyar heavy cavalryman armed with spear and composite bow.
(*Photo and copyright by Nyugati Gyepűk Pajzsa Haditorna Egyesület*)

Magyar heavy cavalryman charging with his two-handed spear.
(*Photo and copyright by Nyugati Gyepűk Pajzsa Haditorna Egyesület*)

of Lothair, died in 875 after having named Carloman – the eldest son of Louis the German – as his heir. His final will, however, was not fully respected, since Charles the Bald was crowned emperor by the pope instead of Carloman and annexed Italy to his dominions.

After several decades of internecine conflict, only two Frankish kingdoms remained: one in the west under Charles the Bald and another in the eastern ruled by Louis the German. In 876, Louis the German died and Charles the Bald tried to occupy the eastern half of the Carolingian realm, but his invasion failed due to the determined opposition of Louis the German's sons. After repelling Charles the Bald's attack, the three sons of Louis the German – Louis the Younger, Carloman of Bavaria and Charles the Fat – divided their father's domains among themselves. In 877, Charles the Bald died and was succeeded by his son, Louis the Stammerer, but he had serious health problems and died after just two years of his rule. The former domains of Charles the Bald were then divided between Louis the Stammerer's two sons: Louis III – who lost the title of emperor – received the territories of northern Gaul, while Carloman was assigned the territories of southern Gaul (becoming known as Carloman of Aquitaine). After Charles the Bald's death, Italy was given to Carloman of Bavaria. However, when he died in 880 without direct heirs, his domains were inherited by his younger brother, Charles the Fat. During 881 and 882, Louis the Younger and Louis III also died without direct heirs, which greatly advantaged

Magyar heavy cavalryman; note the set of armour worn by the horse on the frontal part of the body. (*Photo and copyright by Nyugati Gyepűk Pajzsa Haditorna Egyesület*)

Charles the Fat. Charles annexed the domains of Louis the Younger, while those of Louis III were occupied by Carloman of Aquitaine. In 884, while hunting, Carloman of Aquitaine suffered a mortal wound and died, his extensive territorial possessions in Gaul being annexed by Charles the Fat, who had already held the imperial title since 881. Charles the Fat thus came to control all the Frankish territories in 884 and briefly reunified the Carolingian Empire under his rule.

The closing years of the ninth century saw Frankish territory coming under increasing Viking pressure and a progressive weakening of the central government. The various nobles of the Carolingian realm started to act as independent rulers in their domains, building fortifications without asking permission from the imperial authorities, collecting taxes autonomously and not contributing to the formation of the central army. The socio-political process known as feudalism was developing rapidly across Western Europe, causing a decisive fragmentation of the territorial entities that had emerged during the previous centuries. Individual warlords, ruling from their castles around the countryside, became much more powerful than the central government, which lost most of its original prerogatives, to the advantage of the Church. Charles the Fat died in 888 and left behind a Carolingian Empire that was soon shattered by a new civil war fought between his warlike heirs. By the end of the hostilities, the once solid Frankish Empire had been divided into six smaller realms. Three of these – roughly corresponding to modern France, Germany and Italy – gradually emerged as significant powers. The Kingdom of France was ruled by Count Odo of Paris, who came from a secondary branch of the Carolingians and initiated his own new dynasty, members of which were known as Robertians since they descended from Odo's father, Robert the Strong. Germany came under the control of Arnulf of Carinthia, who was a nephew of Charles the Fat. The Kingdom of Italy, meanwhile, entered a long phase of political chaos: for almost a century, it was ruled by local nobles of Frankish descent, such as Berengar of Friuli and Guy of Spoleto. The semi-Carolingian dynasty of the Robertians governed the Kingdom of France until 987, when the last of its exponents died without heirs and was succeeded by Hugh Capet, who was the eldest son of Count Hugh of Paris and initiated the new dynasty of the Capetians (the term derived from Hugh Capet's nickname, which meant 'cape wearer'). The Carolingians of Germany were extinguished by 911 with the death of Arnulf of Carinthia's son. They were succeeded by the short-lived House of Franconia, which was in turn replaced by the warlike Ottonian dynasty in 919. The Kingdom of Italy remained independent until 951, when it was invaded by the Ottonians. After Charles the Fat's death, the title of Holy Roman Emperor ceased to have any importance until it was assigned to the Ottonians in 962.

While the events described above took place in Western Europe, a new nomadic population of the steppes arrived in Eastern Europe from Central Asia and occupied the lands that had been part of the former Avar Khaganate: the Magyars. They were a confederation of seven tribes, members of which spoke a language belonging to the extensive Finno-Ugrian family. The Magyars probably originated on the territory

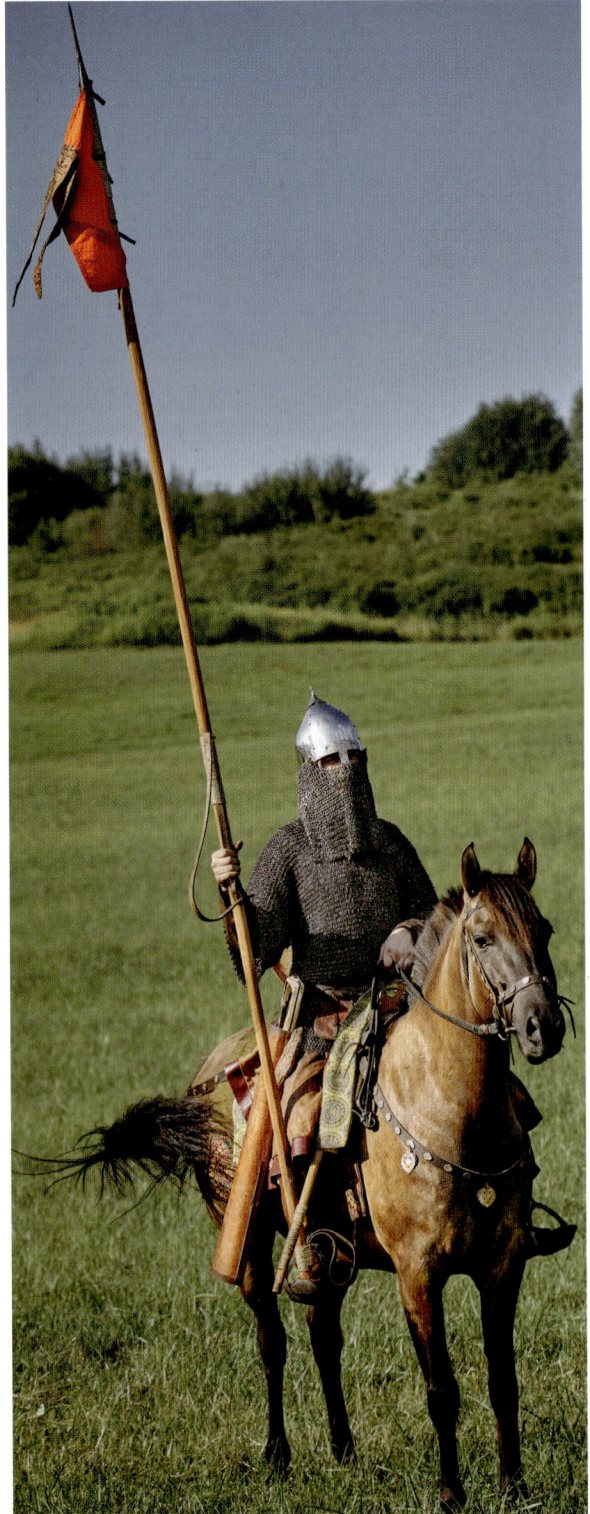

Magyar heavy cavalryman equipped with chainmail; the facial mask attached to the helmet is also made of chainmail. (*Photo and copyright by Nyugati Gyepűk Pajzsa Haditorna Egyesület*)

Magyar heavy cavalryman charging with his two-handed spear.
(*Photo and copyright by Nyugati Gyepűk Pajzsa Haditorna Egyesület*)

of the so-called 'Ugric homeland', which was located in the heart of modern Russia on the European side of the Ural Mountains. From their original settlements, the Magyars migrated westwards, first moving north of the Caspian Sea and then to the Caucasus. From the latter area, they migrated to the Pontic Steppe of Ukraine, following the collapse of the Bulgar state existing on the northern shore of the Black Sea. The seven Magyar tribes, collectively known as Hetumoger, were guided by two supreme leaders who had different functions: the *kende*, who was a sacred religious leader, and the *gyula*, who commanded the fighting forces. After some decades spent in Ukraine, the Magyars migrated to the Carpathian Basin and settled in Pannonia, which following the fall of the Avar Khaganate and the death of Louis the Pious had been the theatre of several conflicts fought between rival powers. The Slavs, who had allied themselves with Charlemagne against the Avars, started to struggle for their independence from the Franks soon after the death of the great Carolingian leader. By 820, they had already created a new Slavic state, which became known as Great Moravia and came to control most of present-day Slovakia and the Czech Republic. The Slavs of Great Moravia became fully independent from the successors of Louis the Pious and started to play an important role in the politics of the Carpathian Basin. To the east of Great Moravia was the heartland of Pannonia, which had been conquered by the Bulgars after the fall of the Avar Khaganate. The Bulgars had

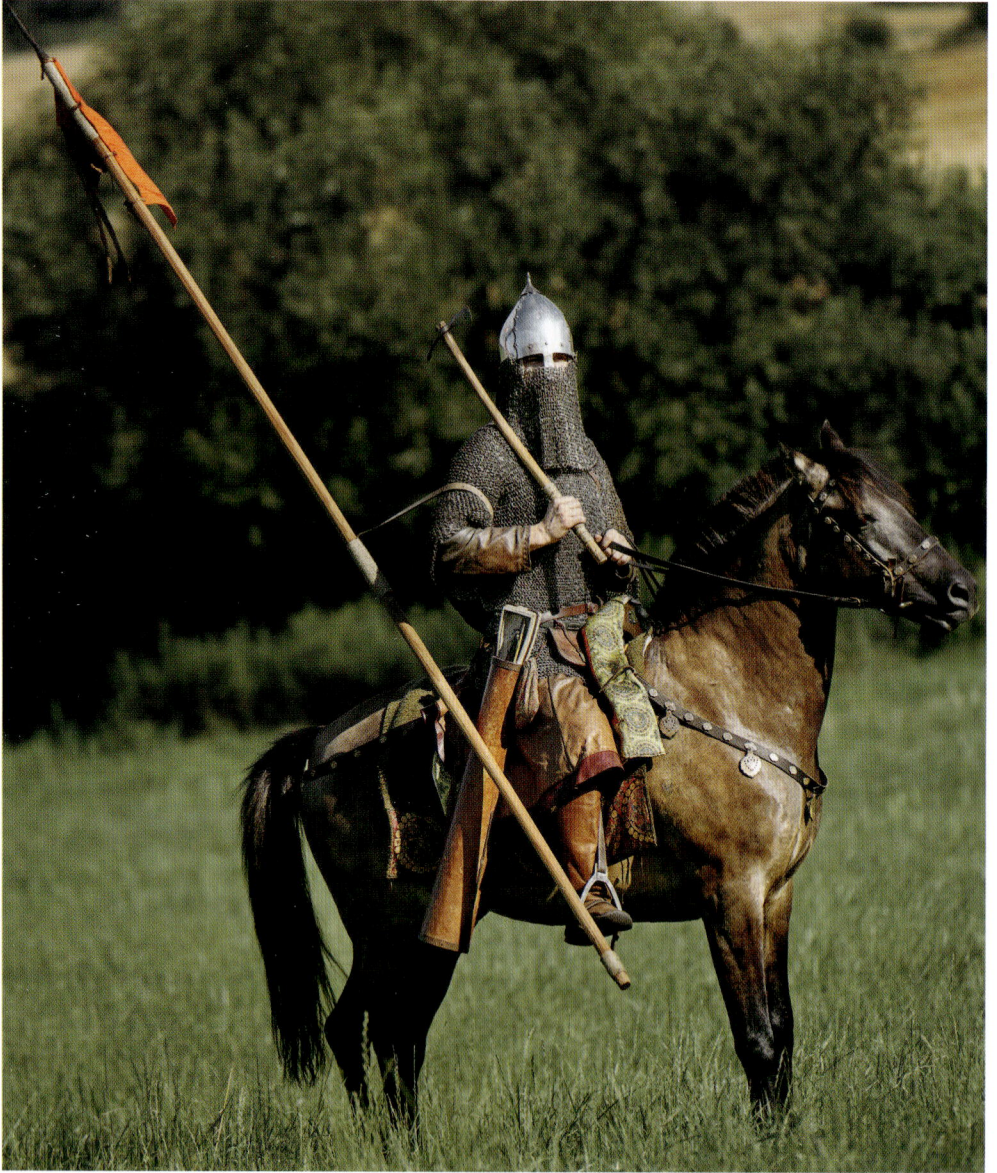

Magyar heavy cavalryman armed with spear, short axe and composite bow.
(*Photo and copyright by Nyugati Gyepűk Pajzsa Haditorna Egyesület*)

long been rivals of the Magyars, especially after the Magyars occupied the plains of Ukraine.

The Magyars' decision to migrate westwards was caused by a series of factors. First of all, they wanted to establish themselves on the rich grasslands of Pannonia in order to have a base from which they could launch raids across Central Europe. Furthermore, they started to come under increasing pressure in Ukraine from another steppe people – the Pechenegs – who were migrating westwards in large numbers. The warlike Magyars appeared for the first time in the Carpathian Basin during 892, when Arnulf of Carinthia invited them to join his forces in the conflict that he was fighting against Great Moravia. The nomadic Magyars responded to the call of Arnulf and crossed the Danube into Pannonia, where they conducted a series of devastating raids against the Slavs. In 894, the Bulgars cut off their diplomatic relations with the Byzantine Empire and invaded its lands, a situation which greatly favoured the Magyars as the Byzantines decided to hire them to fight against the Bulgars, just as Arnulf of Carinthia had done to fight against the Slavs. Arpad and Kurszan, at that time the two supreme leaders of the Magyars, concluded a treaty of alliance with the Byzantine diplomatic envoys and invaded the Bulgar territories in the Balkans. While the Magyars advanced from the north, the Byzantines attacked the Bulgars from the south. The Bulgars soon found themselves in a very difficult situation, being unable to face two powerful enemies at the same time. Consequently, they sent an embassy to the Pechenegs in order to invite them to attack the Magyars from the Pontic Steppe. The diplomatic move of the Bulgars worked well and the Pechenegs invaded Magyar territory from the east. This obliged the Magyars to suspend their offensive against the Bulgars and return to their homeland. Defeated by the Pechenegs, Arpad – who was the supreme commander of the Magyar forces – had no choice but to abandon the last portions of Ukraine that were still under his control. At this point, the Magyars crossed the Carpathian mountain range with the intention of establishing themselves in Pannonia.

Taking advantage of the internal difficulties that Great Moravia was experiencing and of the Bulgars' commitment to the hostilities with the Byzantine Empire, the Magyars rapidly obtained control over part of Pannonia. They renewed their alliance with Arnulf of Carinthia and – on his behalf – raided northern Italy. Arnulf was at the time at war with the King of Italy, Berengar I, which is why the Magyars were sent to plunder a large portion of northern Italy during 899. The first occasion in which military forces of the former Carolingian Empire were routed on the open field by the Magyars happened at the Battle of the Brenta, which saw a crushing defeat inflicted on Berengar's troops. In 900, following Arnulf's death, the Magyars returned to their Pannonian bases, from which they started to complete their conquest of the Carpathian Basin. By 902, Great Moravia had been completely destroyed by the nomads, who submitted all the Slavic tribes living on the territory of modern Hungary. Within a few years, the Magyars consolidated their control over the whole of Pannonia, expelling the Bulgars from the eastern region of their new homeland. A new nomadic state had thus emerged in the heart of Central Europe, which posed a deadly menace for both post-Carolingian Germany and Italy. Soon after consolidating their presence in Pannonia, the Magyars began to conduct regular devastating cavalry raids against both north-eastern Italy and south-eastern Germany (most notably Bavaria and Carinthia). The Magyars had no intention of conquering new lands outside Pannonia, merely conducting these incursions to pillage as many riches as possible. Within a few years they became incredibly rich, none of their enemies having the mobility required to intercept their fast-moving cavalry armies. The tenth century was a time of great trouble for the whole of Europe, due to the activities of three warlike peoples: the Magyars, the Vikings and the Arabs. Whereas the Magyars attacked large areas of Central Europe, the Vikings raided most of Western Europe and the Arabs pillaged the coastline of Mediterranean Europe. It was a very dark period for the continent, which saw the collapse of any form of centralized state as well as the spreading of feudalism and the construction of many castles designed for local defence. The Magyar raids had devastating effects on the economies of several rich territories, including northern Italy, being so frequent that a 'Strada Ungarorum', or 'Route of the Hungarians', was established between Pannonia and Lombardy.

The Magyars arrived in Italy in great numbers during 904, when they were hired by Berengar I to fight against his rival, Louis of Provence, who had assumed control over a significant portion of northern Italy. The Magyars destroyed the military forces of Louis, thus securing victory for Berengar. In exchange for their services, they received permission to pillage all the Italian cities that had sided with Louis of Provence and Berengar agreed to pay them a yearly tribute of about 375kg of silver. In 907, hoping to halt the Magyar incursions into Germany, the Margrave of Bavaria launched an invasion of the Carpathian Basin, but this ended in complete failure with the Germanic troops annihilated by the Magyars at the Battle of Pressburg. A total of nineteen counts, three bishops and three abbots were killed in the clash, which was one of the greatest victories in the history of the Magyars. These events were followed by a devastating incursion against Bavaria, which culminated in another defeat of the Bavarian forces at the Battle of Lengenfeld. Thereafter, the border between Magyar territory and that of Bavaria was fixed on the Enns River. In 908, the Magyars pillaged Thuringia and Saxony, defeating the local Germanic forces at the Battle of Eisenach, which saw the killing of two dukes and one bishop. During 910, the King of Germany, Louis the Child, mobilized his troops against the nomads, but they were crushed at the Battle of Augsburg, following which the Magyars entered Franconia and defeated another large Germanic army at the Battle of Rednitz, with the forces of Franconia, Lotharingia and Bavaria completely annihilated. Louis the Child was left with no choice but to sue for peace, agreeing to pay a tribute to the Magyars. In 911, the Magyar cavalry attacked Swabia and Franconia before crossing the Rhine

Magyar standard-bearer.
(*Photo by Tolnai Turán HSE, copyright by Hungarian Turan Foundation, Tamás Horváth*)

Magyar warrior equipped with corselet of scale armour.
(*Photo by Csongrádi Turán HSE, copyright by Hungarian Turan Foundation, Tamás Horváth*)

Magyar warrior equipped with a full set of lamellar armour. (*Photo by Tolnai Turán HSE, copyright by Hungarian Turan Foundation, Tamás Horváth*)

and plundering Burgundy for the first time. The Magyars raided Saxony again in 915 and reached the Danish border in northern Germany. As the events above clear show, the nomadic Magyar warriors were vastly superior to their Germanic opponents and able to secure any objectives they wanted.

During 919 and 920, the Magyars, having plundered the whole of Germany, turned their eyes to Western Europe, where they attacked Basel and invaded the Duchy of Alsace before transforming Bavaria into a tributary state. In this same period, the Magyars were also active in Eastern Europe, where they supported the Bulgars in their wars against the Byzantines. In 920, a large Magyar army raided most of Germany before entering the Kingdom of France, whose monarch, Charles the Simple, did not have enough troops under his command to face the Magyars on the battlefield and could do little to prevent them plundering his realm. The Magyars, after pillaging much of France, moved to Burgundy, where they crushed the local military forces before invading northern Italy. The years 921–922 saw the Magyars moving freely across Italy, plundering the surroundings of Rome and Naples before attacking Byzantine territories in southern Italy. They returned home during 924 after a plague erupted among their ranks. In 926, Germany was attacked again, together with northern France. The King of Germany was forced to pay a further tribute to the Magyars, who reached the Atlantic Ocean during their incursions. In 933, after forming an alliance with the Pechenegs, the Magyars invaded the Balkans from the north and defeated the Bulgars, who had allied themselves with the Byzantines. The Magyars and the Pechenegs plundered most of the Bulgar lands before heading towards Constantinople. The Byzantines were forced to conclude a peace treaty with the Magyars and to pay them a tribute. In 936, the new King of Germany, Otto I of the new Ottonian dynasty, refused to pay tribute to the Magyars, who responded by attacking and burning the important monastery of Fulda. The raiders, being pagans, showed no respect for the religious sites of their enemies, frequently assaulting them. During 937, the nomads crushed a major French army at Orleans before crossing the whole of France and reaching the Atlantic Ocean. A few months later, they invaded southern Italy and committed widespread plunder, obliging the Abbey of Montecassino to pay them a large tribute. In 942, the Magyars plundered Catalonia and invaded the northern part of Arab Spain, obtaining a series of victories before returning to Italy. In Eastern Europe, the nomads allied themselves with the emerging Kievan Rus during 943 and successfully attacked the Byzantines in the Balkans.

In 954, several German princes rebelled against their king, Otto I, who wanted to transform Germany into a more centralized realm. The rebel aristocrats allied themselves with the Magyars, who sent an army to plunder Bavaria and Swabia. The nomadic troops then went to Worms in order to support the leader of the revolt, Duke

Magyar warrior wearing a helmet with an attached piece of chainmail.
(*Photo by Magyar Turán HSE, copyright by Hungarian Turan Foundation, Tamás Horváth*)

Magyar warrior wearing helmet with an attached piece of chainmail.
(*Photo by Csongrádi Turán HSE, copyright by Hungarian Turan Foundation, Tamás Horváth*)

Magyar warrior wearing a corselet of chainmail; the scabbard is made of ivory.
(*Photo by Csongrádi Turán HSE, copyright by Hungarian Turan Foundation, Tamás Horváth*)

Conrad of Lorraine. From their new base, they plundered large parts of Belgium before crossing most of France and attacking Burgundy. At this time, it was common practice for the Magyars to invade Germany and then cross France before returning to Pannonia via Burgundy and northern Italy. During 955, the nomads decided to support the rebellion of the German aristocrats against Otto I by launching a large attack against south-eastern Germany. They invaded Austria and devastated lands from the Danube to the Black Forest. In order to show the revolting nobles that he was still the legitimate ruler of Germany and that he could protect his realm from a foreign invasion, Otto mobilized all the troops at his disposal and mustered them around Ulm. His intention was to threaten the lines of communications of his enemies, who were now moving north-east towards the important city of Augsburg. The Magyars tried to storm the city but were repulsed due to strong resistance mounted by the local garrison. On 10 August 955, the imperial army of Otto I appeared just south of Augsburg, on the flood plain of the Lech River that was known as Lechfeld. The German monarch commanded eight elite cavalry contingents of professional heavily armed knights: three from Bavaria, two from Swabia and one each from Saxony, Franconia and Bohemia. Otto and his family were from Saxony, and thus the Saxon contingent was the most reliable of the whole army; it was also larger than the others and included the personal guard of the king that was known as the *legio regia*. The Bavarians and Swabians had already fought against the Magyars and were thus experienced knights. The Franconians had revolted against Otto during the previous year but had recently been pardoned, whereas the Bohemians were Slavs, whose home territory was under German political influence. In total, the army of Otto mustered around 9,000 men, each of the cavalry contingents numbering some 1,000 knights, although the Saxons fielded twice that many. The Magyar raiding force, mustering around 10,000–12,000 fighters, consisted almost entirely – as usual – of lightly equipped and fast-moving horse archers.

The Battle of Lechfeld began with a Magyar attack against the imperial rearguard, which comprised the Bohemian contingent. The Bohemians, taken by surprise, were completely routed by the nomads, who continued their assault by attacking the two Swabian contingents. The Swabians suffered severe losses and were unable to protect their army's baggage train. At this point of the battle, however, the Magyars made the mistake of stopping their offensive in order to pillage the German baggage train that they had just captured. Taking advantage of this, Otto grouped his remaining cavalry and launched a massive charge at the head of his elite Saxon contingent. The Magyars, caught off-guard, were forced to engage the enemy in close combat, which they always tried to avoid. The superior training and equipment of the German heavy knights was more than a match for the lightly equipped Magyar archers, who

Magyar warrior equipped with nasal helmet, camail of chainmail and lamellar armour. The general appearance is that of a warrior from the early eleventh century, showing a certain German influence. (*Photo by Tolnai Turán HSE, copyright by Hungarian Turan Foundation, Tamás Horváth*)

Magyar armoured horse archer. The lamellar cuirass is of excellent manufacture.
(*Photo and copyright by Nyugati Gyepűk Pajzsa Haditorna Egyesület*)

were swiftly crushed by Otto's forces. The Germans tried to encircle the Magyars, but without success, the nomads being able to leave the battlefield in good order. During the two days that followed the clash, heavy rainfall and flooding hampered the movements of the Magyar troops, who were intercepted by the German knights

Magyar light cavalryman armed with spear and composite bow.
(*Photo and copyright by Nyugati Gyepűk Pajzsa Haditorna Egyesület*)

while crossing the Lech River and suffered more losses. The Battle of Lechfeld had been a resounding victory for Otto I, who was able to capture the Magyar camp with all the riches contained in it. For the first time in their history, the Magyars had been defeated by the Germans in a major pitched battle: this had a great psychological impact on the German population, which had always considered the Magyars to be invincible warriors. The many Magyars who had been captured at Lechfeld were either executed or mutilated and sent back to their homeland without ears and noses. The defeat shocked the Magyars, who had never before suffered such a severe setback. After defeating the Magyars, Otto I was accepted as monarch by all the German aristocrats and was thus able to pacify his realm. He could also present himself as the defender of Christian Europe, having defeated a powerful pagan enemy. In 962, Otto I went to Rome and was crowned by the pope as Holy Roman Emperor, initiating a new imperial dynasty.

Following the Battle of Lechfeld, the Magyars ceased to conduct incursions across Western Europe and shifted their attention to Eastern Europe. In 957, the Byzantine Empire ceased to pay its yearly tribute to the nomads, which caused a reaction by the Magyars, who invaded the Balkans with a large army two years later. The Magyars plundered a vast area of the Byzantine land up to Constantinople, but on their way back to Pannonia they were intercepted by a Byzantine army and defeated in a night battle. In 961, the Magyars again attacked Byzantine territory, but after raiding Thrace and Macedonia they suffered another setback at the hands of the Byzantines. During 966, they invaded Bulgar lands in the Balkans and forced the Bulgars to make an alliance with them, but this was not enough to change the new balance of power that was emerging in Eastern Europe. The Magyars suffered further defeats in the Balkans in 968, coming to realize that the Byzantines were by now much stronger than they were. They tried to restore their supremacy by forming a new alliance with the Rus of Kiev, but without success. In 970, a large anti-Byzantine army – comprising the Rus of Kiev, Magyars, Bulgars and Pechenegs – invaded the Balkans. However, it was unexpectedly defeated by the Byzantines at the Battle of Arcadiopolis. This setback marked the beginning of a new era in the history of the Magyars, who decided to suspend their raids in Eastern Europe too. Following the Battle of Lechfeld, the Magyar tribes had already started to transform themselves into sedentary groups by establishing new and larger permanent settlements in Pannonia. This process was accelerated from 970, as it became apparent that the only chance of survival for the Magyars was for them to cease being nomadic pagans and instead become sedentary Christians. Two rival factions slowly emerged among the Magyars: one was in favour of the transformation of Pannonia into a Christian realm, with a more centralized government, while the other wanted to continue living in a nomadic way according to the old pagan traditions. In 997, Stephen I, a powerful aristocrat belonging to the pro-Christian faction, became supreme ruler of the Magyars. This caused a wave of malcontent among the nobles who had conservative political ideas, concentrated in the eastern half of the Carpathian Basin and initially not recognizing the legitimacy of Stephen's rule. Hostilities soon broke out between Stephen and his opponents, which lasted for several months. Initially, the pagan faction obtained a series of successes, but Stephen was eventually able to gain the upper hand thanks to the support he received from Emperor Otto III. In the year 1000, Stephen I was crowned King of Hungary with the blessing of Pope Sylvester II – an extremely important political event that marked the birth of a new nation, the Kingdom of Hungary, that would go on to play a prominent role in the history of Eastern Europe. During the following years, most of the Magyars were baptized and Hungary became a Christian realm. Stephen promulgated the first written code of laws of his kingdom and all pagan religious practices were discontinued. By 1003, Stephen I had consolidated his control over all the Magyar lands, meaning Hungarian territory could start to be organized according to the contemporary feudal model that was already dominant in Central Europe. The nomadic history of the Magyars had come to an end.

The Magyar forces, differently from those of the Avars, consisted of large cavalry contingents that were entirely made up of lightly equipped and fast-moving horse archers. According to the latest archaeological finds, no separate body of Magyar heavy cavalry existed, only a few of the richest Magyar nobles being equipped with corselets of lamellar armour. The Magyar armies that pillaged most of Europe during the tenth century did not comprise any infantry contingents, as they had to move very rapidly from one place to another in order to avoid direct confrontations with their pursuing enemies. The Magyars, like all the nomadic peoples of the steppes, were masters in employing effective light cavalry tactics. Indeed, the scouting and skirmishing of their horse archers were unrivalled, and they were also capable of organizing deadly ambushes thanks to their use of elusive tactics such as feigned retreats. Speed was the key factor behind their victories, together with the excellent quality of their mounts. As already mentioned, the Magyars were a confederation of seven tribes, or hordes, each of which comprised a different number of clans. All able-bodied Magyar males were warriors and had to fight for their clan when called to do so. The supreme religious leader of the Magyar tribes, the *kende*, had at his disposal a large bodyguard provided by the Kavars. These were not ethnic Magyars, instead being – at least initially – mercenaries of Turkic stock. They joined the Magyars after they had settled in Pannonia and apparently provided elite bodyguards of mercenaries to several prominent Magyar warlords. Differently from the Avars, the Magyars did not use significant numbers of auxiliary infantrymen provided by the

Magyar horse archer firing his composite bow.
(*Photo and copyright by Nyugati Gyepűk Pajzsa Haditorna Egyesület*)

Magyar horse archer. The whip was often used as a secondary weapon during close combat by the warriors of the nomadic peoples. (*Photo and copyright by Nyugati Gyepűk Pajzsa Haditorna Egyesület*)

peoples they had submitted in the Carpathian Basin. On some occasions, however, they were supported by contingents of Slavic foot troops. When the Magyars settled in Pannonia, there were still sizeable communities of Avars living in the east of the region. The Magyars decided not to destroy the Avars, and instead progressively absorbed them into their social organization. The heirs of the last Avar groups living in Pannonia became known as Székely and developed their own peculiar culture that

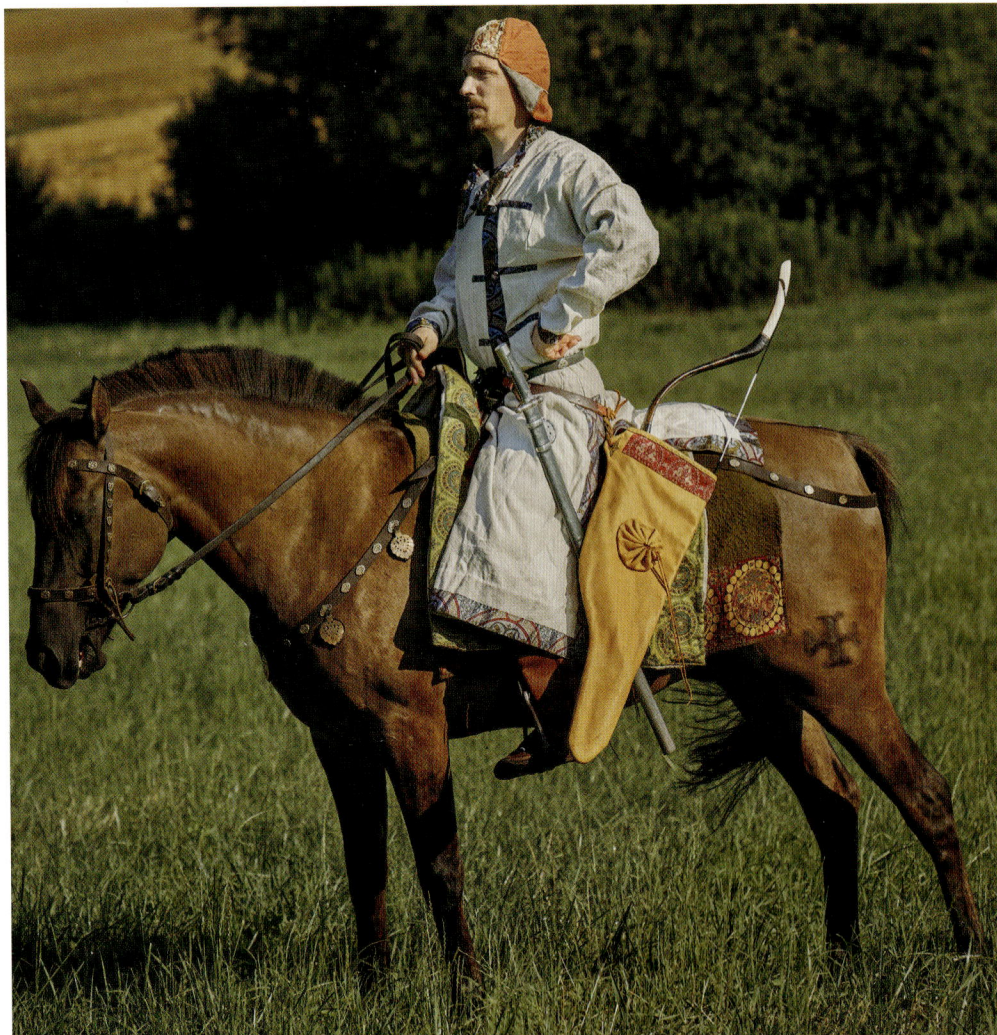

Magyar horse archer. (*Photo and copyright by Nyugati Gyepűk Pajzsa Haditorna Egyesület*)

was strongly influenced by the Magyars. Apparently, the Magyar leaders entrusted the Székely with the defence of the eastern frontiers of Pannonia, employing them as auxiliaries on several occasions while fighting against the Byzantines.

Magyar light cavalry were equipped quite similarly to those of the Avars. Most Magyar horse archers wore a tall pointed cap that usually had earflaps and was trimmed with fur. The cap was sometimes replaced with a pointed metal helmet, which usually had an attached piece of chainmail on the back that was designed to protect the neck. The universal Magyar helmet was segmented and quite tall. The standard Magyar tunic was very similar to that used by the Avars, being knee-length and loose fitting. It could have rich decorations on the external edges and

Magyar saddle. (*Photo and copyright by Nyugati Gyepűk Pajzsa Haditorna Egyesület*)

was often trimmed with fur on the collar or around the cuffs. The tunics of the aristocrats could be made of silk and have complex embroidering. Over the tunic, especially during colder months, Magyar warriors wore a long topcoat that had the same basic features as the tunic and usually had side-vents since it was designed for riding. Magyar trousers were quite baggy and were worn tucked into comfortable leather boots. The Magyars wore their hair long and shaved their chins, differently from other steppe peoples. Their clothes were often decorated with symbols taken from their pagan religion, such as the black raven that was distinctive of the royal family initiated by Arpad. The Magyar composite bow had the same basic features as the Avar one, being extremely effective from medium distances. It was carried in a specific case, which was used together with a quiver that was very similar to that employed by the Huns. In addition to their bow, most Magyar warriors were also armed with a light spear and a small axe or hammer. Each Magyar warrior also had a sword, which was single-edged and had a slightly curved blade. A short dagger, with a curved blade, was usually carried in the waistbelt. Magyar horse equipment did not include any protective element, but comprised a wood-framed saddle very similar to that used by the Avars. By the time of Stephen I's coronation, the military equipment of the Magyars had started to change considerably, with a number of Magyar horsemen beginning to be equipped similarly to the German feudal knights.

They wore chainmail with short sleeves and started to use swords having straight blades as well as round shields painted with decorative motifs. As a result of these changes, the tribal cavalry consisting of mounted archers was gradually replaced by a feudal cavalry made up of heavy knights. The Kavars were replaced as bodyguards of the most prominent nobles by German mercenary knights, but the Székely continued to serve as horse archers on the eastern frontiers of Hungary.

Chapter 5

The Bulgars, 630–1241

The Bulgars arrived in the steppes north of the Sea of Azov around the late sixth century AD. They belonged to the Turkic linguistic family and had many characteristics in common with the Turkic peoples, who had become a prominent military power of the Eurasian steppes following the decline of the White Huns. After coming under increasing pressure from the migrating Khazars, the tribes making up the Bulgar people were forced to divide into two groups and to leave their homeland around 668. One group migrated westwards to the Danube area and slowly established itself on the territory of present-day Bulgaria in the Balkans; the other group moved north and went to the plains located between the Kama River and the Upper Volga region. The Bulgars who migrated to the Balkans gradually mixed with the local Slavic communities and abandoned their own Turkic language to adopt a new southern Slavic one. They also embraced the Orthodox Christian faith and progressively created a substantial Balkan state that fought many bloody wars against the Byzantine Empire. The Bulgars who moved north, known as Volga Bulgars, established themselves on a flourishing territory covered by forests and fertile valleys that had been inhabited by Finno-Ugrian tribes for a long time. They created a form of nomadic state that was submitted – albeit only formally – to the Khazars until the latter were defeated by the Kievan Rus in 965. Very little is known about the early state that the Bulgars established north of the Sea of Azov, which existed as a unified political entity during the period 630–668. It was known as Old Great Bulgaria, or Patria Onoguria, and was a confederation comprising several Bulgar tribes. This early Bulgar state established positive diplomatic relations with the Byzantine Empire and, as we have seen, rivalled the Avar Khaganate for control of the Ukrainian plains. In 668, however, Old Great Bulgaria disintegrated under the increasing military pressure of the Khazars, who were establishing themselves in the Pontic Steppe and were much more numerous than the Bulgars.

The Bulgars who migrated westwards to the Balkans occupied the region of modern Bessarabia and established themselves in the Danube Delta. A few years later, they crossed the great river and entered the Byzantine province of Scythia Minor, the steppe grasslands and pastures of which were fundamental for the survival of the large herd stocks of the Bulgars. The Byzantines organized a military expedition against the nomadic newcomers in 680, but this ended in disaster for Emperor Constantine IV, who was defeated at the Battle of Onglos on the Danube Delta. Following their victory, the Bulgars advanced south and invaded Thrace, forcing the Byzantines to sign a humiliating peace treaty in 681, according to which the Byzantine Empire recognized Bulgaria as an independent state and agreed to pay a yearly tribute to it. This was the first time the Byzantines legally surrendered claims to part of their Balkan dominions, an act of great historical importance. Once in their new homeland, the Bulgars rapidly submitted the large communities of Slavs who lived inside the borders of the Byzantine Empire and had migrated to the Balkans during the Avar invasions of Byzantine lands. The Bulgars, with their large cavalry forces, were far too powerful for the Slavs, and like the Avars before them, the nomadic newcomers transformed the Slavic communities into vassals and started to cooperate with them against the Byzantines. The Slavs were allowed to retain their chiefs and their customs, in return for which they had to pay tribute in kind and provide auxiliary foot soldiers to the Bulgars. The Bulgars relocated most of the Slavic tribes to the western frontier of their new homeland in order to protect it from the Avars; just one Slavic tribe was sent to the eastern parts of the Balkan Mountains to guarding the passes that connected Bulgaria with the Byzantine Empire. Once in the Balkans, the Bulgars continued to fight against the Khazars, but suffered some setbacks. Despite this, however, they consolidated their presence in Bulgaria and temporarily improved their relations with the Byzantines by signing a new treaty with them in 716.

When the Arabs laid siege to Constantinople from 717–718, the Bulgars sent a large army to the city in order to support the Byzantines. According to contemporary sources, they played a decisive role in the subsequent defeat of the Arabs, killing more than 20,000 Muslim soldiers in battle. During the mid-eighth century, Bulgaria experienced a series of political troubles, which produced great internal instability. Several Bulgar leaders were assassinated and the state lived in a condition of anarchy for many years. Two opposing factions emerged among the Bulgars: one favoured maintaining positive relations with the Byzantines, while the other wanted to invade all Byzantine lands and conquer Constantinople. The internal divisions of the Bulgars were used to his advantage by Emperor Constantine V, who launched nine major campaigns against them. Despite being able to defeat the Bulgars on several occasions, the Byzantines could not retake the territory of Bulgaria and failed to impose a lasting peace. The devastations of Bulgar lands ordered by Constantine V made the alliance between Bulgars and Slavs even more solid, while only serving to increase the Bulgars' dislike of the Byzantines. In 792, a Bulgar army crushed Byzantine forces at the Battle of Marcellae, after which the Byzantine Empire was again forced to pay an annual tribute to the Bulgar leaders, or khans. During the early ninth century, Bulgaria

Bulgar armoured horse archer wearing pointed helmet with attached piece of chainmail. (*Photo by Jasmin Parvanov, copyright by Equestrian Martial Arts School – Madara Horseman, Obzor, Bulgaria, and Association for Restoration and Preservation of Bulgarian Traditions – Avitohol, Varna, Bulgaria*)

Cumans represented a deadly threat to the important trade routes that connected Kiev with Constantinople across the Black Sea and the Balkans. During 1180–1183, however, the Russian principalities that had emerged from the collapse of the Kievan Rus started to collaborate against the nomads and achieved some significant victories over the Cumans. Nevertheless, the Cumans continued to fight successfully in the Balkans for several more decades, as allies of the Second Bulgarian Empire and against the Byzantine Empire. Without the decisive military support of the Cumans, the Bulgars would have never regained their independence from the Byzantines. The Cumans remained loyal allies of the new Bulgar state for several decades and contributed to its survival, even after the Byzantine Empire was partitioned between the crusaders from Western Europe who took Constantinople during the Fourth Crusade in 1204. When the crusaders tried to invade the Second Bulgarian Empire, the Cumans provided 14,000 horse archers to their Bulgar allies and helped them win a decisive victory against the western knights at the Battle of Adrianople in 1205. By the beginning of the thirteenth century, the Cumans had established a solid presence both east and south of the Carpathian Mountains, controlling large parts

Bulgar heavy cavalryman equipped with sabre and round shield. (*Photo by Dimitar Atanasov, copyright by Association for Restoration and Preservation of Bulgarian Traditions – Avitohol, Varna, Bulgaria*)

Bulgar heavy cavalryman wearing corselet of chainmail. (*Photo by Dean Nedialkov, copyright by Bulgarian School of Ancient Military Arts – Greatness, Varna, Bulgaria*)

doubled in size by occupying vast regions located along the Middle Danube. As we have seen, the Bulgars contributed to the disintegration of the Avar Khaganate by conquering their eastern territory. They also established a border with the Frankish Empire along the Tisza River and penetrated into Byzantine Macedonia. In 811, Emperor Nicephorus I tried to limit the Bulgars' expansion by launching a massive counter-offensive, resulting in the Byzantines plundering and burning down the Bulgars' capital of Pliska. While marching back to their bases, however, the Byzantine troops were ambushed and decisively defeated by the Bulgars at the Battle of Varbitsa Pass. Nicephorus I was killed during the battle and his skull was later used as a drinking cup by the Bulgar khan, Krum, who had defeated him. After failed peace talks, the Bulgars invaded Thrace and prepared to capture Constantinople, but in April 814, however, they suspended hostilities due to the sudden death of their leader, Krum.

Subsequently, there was a period of peace between the Bulgars and the Byzantines, the Bulgars being content to consolidate their significantly expanded territorial possessions. In the south-west, Bulgar lands reached the modern city of Belgrade, while in the north-west they bordered with the Frankish Empire along the Danube. In the north-east, the frontier between Bulgar territories and those of the Khazars was marked by the Dnieper River. It was during this period that the Bulgars gradually transformed themselves into a sedentary people, exactly like the Magyars did almost two centuries later in Pannonia. They formulated their first written code of laws and remodelled the nomadic settlement of Pliska as a proper city with permanent buildings. Bulgar expansion into the southern Balkans resumed during the central decades of the ninth century, which saw Bulgaria reaching the Adriatic Sea near Valona thanks to the conquest of Macedonia. The Byzantines, at the time being extremely weak militarily, could do little to stop the advance of the Bulgars. Constantinople favoured the development of a new Slavic state placed under its political patronage, the Principality of Serbia, but this was not capable of limiting the Bulgars' expansionism. In 864, khan Boris I converted to Christianity and established a Bulgarian Orthodox Church that was fully independent from both Constantinople and Rome. He also sponsored the use of the Bulgarian language in all the written documents of his realm. The late ninth century saw the Byzantines forming an alliance with the Magyars against the Bulgars, who responded by allying themselves with the Pechenegs. In 896, a Byzantine army was routed at the decisive Battle of Boulgarophygon, but Constantinople was able to gradually recover from this setback and resumed hostilities against the Bulgars. During 917, the Bulgars prevailed again in the major Battle of Acheolus, which resulted in Bulgaria's total military supremacy in the Balkans. A few years later, in 924, the Bulgars defeated and conquered the Principality of Serbia.

Bulgar warrior wearing pointed helmet with an attached piece of chainmail.
(*Photo by Dean Nedialkov, copyright by Bulgarian School of Ancient Military Arts – Greatness, Varna, Bulgaria*)

Bulgar warrior wearing short-sleeved corselet of chainmail.
(*Photo by Dean Nedialkov, copyright by Bulgarian School of Ancient Military Arts – Greatness, Varna, Bulgaria*)

Bulgar aristocratic warrior. (*Photo by Dimitar Atanasov, copyright by Association for Restoration and Preservation of Bulgarian Traditions – Avitohol, Varna, Bulgaria*)

By 927, Bulgaria was enjoying a 'golden age', the Byzantine Empire having lost control over most of the Balkan territories except for Greece and the immediate surroundings of Constantinople. After a lengthy string of defeats, the Byzantines were forced to recognize the khan as Emperor of Bulgaria and to accept the independence of the Bulgarian Orthodox Church. Bulgaria then lived in peace until 968, a period that was characterized by political consolidation and economic expansion. This situation changed only with the emergence of the Kievan Rus as a significant military power in Eastern Europe, which altered the balance of power that had been established in 927. Between 968 and 970, having been invited to do so by the Byzantines, the Kievan Prince Svyatoslav I invaded Bulgaria at the head of a large army. This defeated the Bulgars and captured their new capital of Preslav. The unexpected success of the Kievan Rus caused great concern in Constantinople and led to a confrontation between Svyatoslav and the Byzantines. Against all odds, the forces of Constantinople prevailed and forced the Kievan Rus to leave the Balkans in 971. The campaigns of 968–971 devastated large portions of Bulgaria and allowed the Byzantines to reconquer – albeit temporarily – the western Bulgar lands. However, the Bulgars were soon able to reorganize themselves and recover all the territories that they had lost. They even expanded southwards by conquering some regions of Greece – including Thessaly and Epirus – that they had never controlled before. The power of Bulgaria was fully restored, aided by the establishment of a strong alliance with Stephen I of Hungary. This situation, however, did not last for long, with the new Byzantine Emperor Basil II launching annual campaigns from the year 1000 that methodically seized Bulgar strongholds. The war of attrition between Bulgars and Byzantines dragged on until 1014, when the Bulgars were decisively defeated at the Battle of Kleidion. This clash resulted in the capture of 14,000 Bulgars, and it is said that 99 out of every 100 Bulgar captives were blinded by the Byzantines in order to prevent a Bulgarian resurgence. Due to this victory and his incredible cruelty, Basil II was nicknamed Bulgaroktonos, or 'Bulgar Slayer'. Four years after the Battle of Kleidion, the whole of Bulgaria was annexed to the Byzantine Empire and the history of the First Bulgarian Empire came to an end. The Bulgars regained their independence only in 1185 with the establishment of the Second Bulgarian Empire, but this was a state that no longer had any nomadic features.

The Volga Bulgars, after migrating northwards and settling in the Middle Volga region, started exerting dominance over the local Finno-Ugrian communities, just as the other Bulgars did with the Slavs in the Balkans. Commanding the Volga River in its middle course, the new nomadic state established by the Bulgars in Russia controlled much of the trading activities that took place between Europe and Asia. The Volga Bulgars soon became extremely rich thanks to commerce and established

Bulgar warrior wearing fur cap.
(*Photo by Dimitar Atanasov, copyright by Bulgarian School of Ancient Military Arts – Greatness, Varna, Bulgaria*)

Bulgar horse archer equipped with composite bow. (*Photo by Dimitar Atanasov, copyright by Association for Restoration and Preservation of Bulgarian Traditions – Avitohol, Varna, Bulgaria*)

Bulgar armoured horse archer. (*Photo by Jasmin Parvanov, copyright by Equestrian Martial Arts School – Madara Horseman, Obzor, Bulgaria, and Association for Restoration and Preservation of Bulgarian Traditions – Avitohol, Varna, Bulgaria*)

an impressive capital at Bolghar. They traded with the Vikings, who were extremely active on the major Russian rivers, but also with the Byzantines and the Arabs. Initially, the Volga Bulgars paid tribute to the Khazars, but they eventually grew so much in size and power that they gradually freed themselves from the political influence of the Khazarian Khaganate. In 965, the Khaganate was destroyed by the expanding Kievan Rus and the Volga Bulgars became fully independent. During the following decades, however, they had to fight several campaigns against the Kievan Rus in order to preserve the survival of their state. In 985, having been unable to crush the Volga Bulgars, the Kievan Rus signed a peace treaty with the nomads that recognized their full independence. This treaty was respected for almost a century and led to the establishment of positive commercial relations between the Volga Bulgars and the Kievan Rus. Meanwhile, since 922, the Volga Bulgars had converted to Islam, like other steppe peoples before them (notably the Turks). During the twelfth century, the Volga Bulgars fought several wars against the Russian principalities that emerged after the collapse of the Kievan Rus. These conflicts lasted for more than a century but proved indecisive for the Russians, whose attempted invasions of Bulgar lands all ended in failure. In 1223, the Mongols of Genghis Khan appeared on the borders of the Bulgar territories, marking the beginning of a new era in the history of the Russian steppes. Initially, the Volga Bulgars were able to contain the incursions of the Mongols, but in 1236 their forces were finally destroyed by the invaders. By 1241, all the Bulgar settlements in the Volga region had been destroyed by the Mongols, who annexed Volga Bulgaria to their expanding empire.

The Bulgars who migrated to the Balkans were not particularly numerous but could deploy a sizeable number of elite cavalrymen, who proved more than a match for the local Slavic communities. The Bulgar cavalry mostly consisted of armoured horsemen armed with spear and composite bow, who, similarly to the Avar heavy cavalry, were capable of conducting frontal charges as well as of operating as horse archers. As a result, there was no clear separation in the Bulgar nomadic cavalry between heavy horsemen and lightly equipped mounted archers, since most of the warriors wore armour but employed the composite bow of the steppes as their primary weapon. The various aristocratic Bulgar warlords were tasked with commanding the cavalry contingents, which were recruited and organized on a clan basis. Each noble had his own personal retinue of well-equipped warriors, just like the supreme ruler or khan, who could count on an elite personal bodyguard of professional soldiers who served on a permanent basis and were still paid in peacetime. After submitting the Slavic communities of their new Balkan homeland, the Bulgars increased their forces by absorbing large numbers of Slavic light infantrymen into their troops. With the progression of time, the Bulgar armies started to consist of a relatively small elite cavalry made up of nomads and a large infantry force comprising Slavs. The cavalry was tasked with deciding the outcome of pitched battles, while the infantry performed siege operations and protected the frontiers from enemy attacks. With the gradual transformation of the Bulgars into a sedentary people, the cavalry assumed an increasingly aristocratic nature, representing the social elite that dominated the vast Slavic population of commoners. The Bulgars provided the commanding officers for the foot units made up of Slavs and continued to act as the backbone of Bulgaria's military forces until the First Bulgarian Empire disappeared. At the peak of its power, the First Bulgarian Empire could deploy 30,000 fully equipped heavy cavalrymen, whose horses were all armoured. These elite warriors operated as part of a very effective defensive system that was designed to deal with the frequent Byzantine invasions. Several strong fortifications were erected across the territory of Bulgaria, which acted as bases for the cavalry contingents as well as important commercial centres. The Bulgars paid particular attention to preserving the excellent quality of their mounts, for example by conducting frequent inspections of the horses. On the battlefield, they often concentrated sizeable numbers of extra horses behind their main combat formations, in order to have fresh mounts in case of need as well as to prevent surprise attacks from the rear. Despite being heavily equipped, the Bulgar heavy cavalrymen were masters at organizing ambushes and performing feigned retreats. They were capable of riding while turning backwards and firing clouds of arrows on any pursuing enemies. The forces of the Volga Bulgars had more or less the same organization as those deployed by the First Bulgarian Empire. Their core was made up by the professional heavy cavalrymen, who were divided into two distinct categories according to their seniority. The khan commanded an elite bodyguard of 500 mounted warriors and the large auxiliary infantry force was provided by the several Finno-Ugrian tribes that had been submitted by the Volga Bulgars. The Finno-Ugrian infantry comprised both heavily equipped foot soldiers and lightly equipped skirmishers.

The equipment of the combatants was more or less the same for both the Bulgars of the Balkans and the Bulgars of the Volga. Bulgar helmets could be of two different kinds: one had a sphero-conical form and directly riveted plate construction, with a long tube for a plume and a long protective nasal bar, while the other also had a sphero-conical form but a rectangular cut-out above the face, which was covered by a face mask serving as a protective visor. Bulgar armour comprised both chainmail and corselets of scale armour, which were frequently used in combination. The mail shirts were quite short compared with those produced in Western Europe and were short-sleeved. The corselets of scale armour could have *lamellae* of either iron or leather. In most cases, a Bulgar cavalryman wore a corselet of iron scale armour over a short mail

Bulgar warrior equipped with round shield.
(*Photo by Dean Nedialkov, copyright by Bulgarian School of Ancient Military Arts – Greatness, Varna, Bulgaria*)

Bulgar noble warrior of the
Second Bulgarian Empire.
(*Photo and copyright by Boris
Bedrosov, Burgas, Bulgaria*)

Bulgar heavy infantryman from the late thirteenth century (Second Bulgarian Empire). The whole equipment shows a clear Byzantine influence. (*Photo by Dimitar Atanassov, IEFSEM-BAS, Experiencing History Research Project, copyright by Kalina Atanasova, https:// badamba.info/, Bulgaria*)

shirt. Bulgar shields were round and light, with a hemispherical boss over a central hole, behind which was quite a long grip bar. The Bulgars transported their armour and shields inside special bags loaded on horse-drawn vehicles while travelling, in order to protect them from the changing weather conditions. Their belts were more important than armour, reflecting the social position of their wearer. Bulgar belts were often decorated with golden, silver, bronze or copper elements. All the Bulgar warriors were armed with a light sabre that had a curved blade, which was designed for mounted use. This had a long and narrow blade that tapered smoothly towards the point. The steel crossguards of such weapons often had down-sloping quillons with ball- or diamond-shaped terminals and flattened sides (which provided good protection to the user's hand). The scabbards of sabres were made of wood and had a leather covering, along with decorated bronze chapes (tips), lockets and mounts for straps. The Bulgar cavalrymen wielded effective spears designed to pierce armour, as well as other offensive weapons that were of great use in hand-to-hand fighting (including battleaxes, maces and bludgeons). The Bulgar composite bow had the same basic features as that employed by the Avars.

Chapter 6

The Khazars and the Alans, 550–1239

The Khazars emerged as a significant military power of the Eurasian steppes around AD 550. They had Turkic origins like the Bulgars and established themselves over a significant area of the Caucasus. Within a few decades they became increasingly numerous and powerful, launching a series of devastating incursions against the Sasanian Empire and causing the collapse of Old Great Bulgaria around 668. The Sasanians were forced to build massive fortifications on their northern borders in order to limit the military activities of the nomadic Khazars, who slowly started to have good diplomatic relations with the Byzantine Empire. When the Byzantines fought their last and decisive conflict against the Sasanians in the Middle East (602–628), under the leadership of Emperor Heraclius, the Khazars sided with them and played a significant role in the war that destroyed most of the Sasanian military power. The central decades of the seventh century were a time of great change for the Middle East, seeing the rapid ascendancy of the Arabs and their new Muslim faith. Taking advantage of the weakness of both the Byzantines and the Sasanians, who had fought against each other for decades, the Arabs conquered most of the Middle East in just a few years. The new military superpower that emerged from these campaigns, the Islamic Caliphate, soon challenged the power of the Khazars in the Caucasus. Initially, the Khazars were able to repulse the Muslim incursions into the Caucasus, but during 713 the Arabs raided deep into Khazaria. A few years later, in 721, Islamic forces mounted a full-scale invasion of Khazarian lands and conquered the capital, Balanjar. The following years saw strong resistance by the nomads against the Arab invaders, which blocked Muslim expansion into the Caucasus. In 731, the Khazars conducted an effective counter-offensive against the Arabs, which expelled the Muslims from most of the Caucasus and even reached northern Iraq before being halted. Subsequently, the Khazars confirmed their historical alliance with the Byzantines in order to count on a powerful ally that could cooperate with them against the Caliphate. Around 740, as part of their anti-Muslim resistance, the Khazars abandoned their traditional pagan faith and converted to Judaism. This differentiated the cultural identity of the Khazars from that of all the other peoples of the steppes, since they were the only nomads to embrace Judaism.

Khazar heavy cavalryman
wearing lamellar armour.
(*Photo and copyright by
Skjaldborg Vikings*)

Khazar warrior equipped with pointed helmet having an attached piece of chainmail. (*Photo by Hrafn Vaeringi, copyright by Amy Nicklin Photography*)

Khazar heavy cavalryman equipped with full set of lamellar armour. The whole panoply shows a certain Byzantine influence. (*Photo by Hrafn Vaeringi, copyright by Amy Nicklin Photography*)

The ninth century was an age of consolidation for the Khazarian state in the Caucasus, which came to control most of the Pontic Steppe in Ukraine and stabilized the frontier with the Caliphate around Derbent. Conflicts between the Khazars and the Arabs continued for several more decades, but they were – on most occasions –

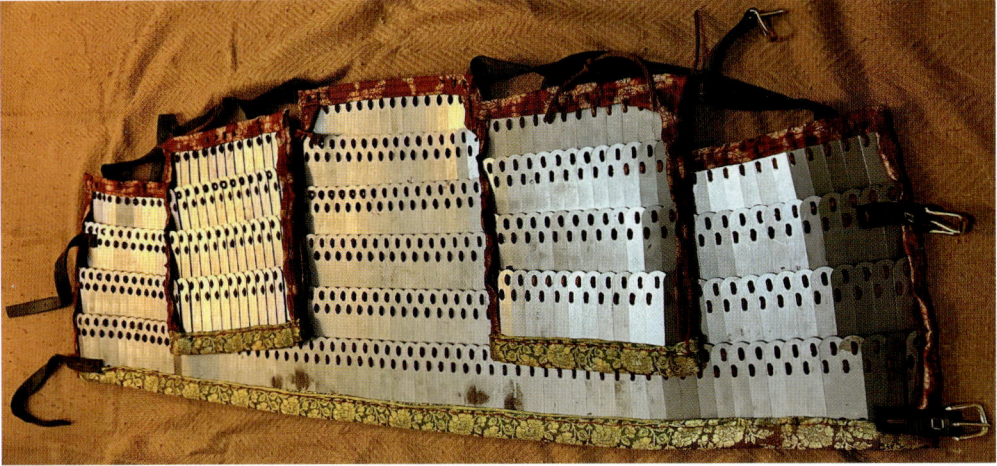

Khazar corselet of lamellar armour. (*Photo and copyright by Skjaldborg Vikings*)

low-intensity border wars that consisted of raids and skirmishes. Thanks to this period of relative stability, the Khazarian Khaganate was able to emerge as a significant regional power of Eurasia that rivalled the Byzantine Empire for dominance over various regions around the Black Sea, including Crimea. The mid-tenth century saw the ascendancy of the Kievan Rus, a new state that rapidly came to dominate most of Russia and Ukraine. The Kievan Rus was created by the Varangians (the Eastern Vikings), who – by moving on the great rivers of Eastern Europe – migrated from Scandinavia and submitted the large Slavic communities living in the region. By mixing with the Slavs, the Varangians were able to create a strong unified state that had its capital in Kiev (which had been founded as a Khazarian settlement). In 909, the Eastern Vikings conducted their first incursion against Khazarian territory, which was followed by a larger one in 913 and 914. The Kievan Rus gradually became increasingly powerful and started to plan the complete destruction of the Khazarian Khaganate, which controlled the main commercial routes that crossed both the Black Sea and the Caucasus. The Khazars obliged the Slavic communities living on their borders to pay tributes and could close the course of the Volga River to foreign merchants, both of which were unacceptable to the Varangians, who were in the process of becoming the overlords of the Slavic communities and the leading merchants of the Pontic Steppe. In 965, Svyatoslav I of Kievan Rus launched a massive invasion of the Khazarian lands, which ended in 969 with complete victory for the Varangians. By 985, what remained of Khazarian territory had been partitioned between the Kievan Rus and the Muslim state of Khwarazam. The history of the Khazarian Khaganate thus came to an end and most of the surviving Khazarians were forced to convert to Islam.

The Alans probably originated from the fusion of some eastern Sarmatian groups with those of the Massagetae. After entering the Pontic Steppe during the first century BC, they soon became the dominant military power of the region and gradually replaced the Sarmatians. Until the beginning of the Great Migrations of the Germanic peoples, the Alans exerted their military dominance over what remained of the Sarmatians (who were partly absorbed by the Alans) and fought several campaigns against the Roman Empire. Around AD 250, the migrating Goths started to exert increasing pressure on the frontiers of the Alan lands, a situation that continued until the Germanic communities were finally able to defeat the Alans and conquer the Pontic Steppe. It should be noted, however, that after the initial clashes, the nomads and the newcomers established positive relations between themselves in order to achieve some common goals. The Goths learned from the Alans how to ride horses and how to fight from horseback, whereas the Alans were able to improve their metal-working skills thanks to their cooperation with the Germanic communities. With the ascendancy of the Huns in the early years of the fifth century, both the Alans and the Goths lost their prominence in the Pontic Steppe and became vassals of the Hunnic Empire. As such, they participated in the bloody campaigns fought by Attila against the Western Roman Empire, which eventually caused its final collapse. Since the fourth century, the Alans had become closely associated with the Goths, to the point that some of them participated in the Gothic westward migration that culminated with the decisive Battle of Adrianople in 378. Before the Huns' ascendancy in Eastern Europe, the Alans had split themselves into two groups: many of them remained in the steppes located north of the Caucasus, while others joined the Germanic Vandals in their migration. The Alans who associated themselves with the Vandals crossed the Rhine and entered the territory of Gaul, where they established a realm of their own. This group, as we have seen, cooperated with the Romans of Flavius Aetius against the Huns and deployed a significant military contingent at the Battle of the Catalaunian Fields. Following victory in this clash, the Alans remained in Gaul for some time and established their capital at Orleans. During the 460s, they had to defend their new homeland from the assaults of the Visigoths and the Franks. Over time, however, it became apparent that the Germanic peoples were much stronger militarily than the Alans, who were left with no choice but to accept the suzerainty of the Franks. Meanwhile, those of the Alans who had remained with the Vandals migrated with them into the Iberian peninsula. Here, the Alans established a small but flourishing kingdom, which survived until being invaded and destroyed by the Visigoths in 418. Following these events, the surviving Alans moved to North Africa with the Vandals, which marked the end of their separate ethnic identity as they were rapidly absorbed by their Germanic allies.

Khazar corselet of scale armour. (*Photo and copyright by Skjaldborg Vikings*)

The Alans who remained in the Caucasus had a much longer history than those who migrated westwards. They established an independent nomadic state known as Alania that extended from the Kuban River in the west to the Darial Gorge in the east. With the ascendancy of the Khazarian Khaganate, the Alans became their vassals of the latter and Alania subsequently acted as an important buffer state during the bloody Khazar-Arab Wars. The Alans were longstanding loyal allies of the Khazars until becoming fully independent from them in the late ninth century. During the following decades, Alania came under strong Byzantine political influence, which led to the Alans' conversion to Orthodox Christianity. Following the downfall of Khazaria, the Alans confirmed their alliance with the Byzantines because their lands were being menaced by the expansionism of steppe peoples such as the Pechenegs and the Kipchaks. By the time of their religious conversion, the Alans had become a sedentary people and their realm in the Caucasus was strongly influenced by the Byzantine Empire. The independent history of the Alans came to an end during the 1230s, when the Mongols invaded the Caucasus. By 1239, the whole of Alania had been conquered by Genghis Khan's successors.

The Khazars, similarly to the Magyars, were ruled by two supreme leaders: one was tasked with managing and commanding the military forces, while the other performed a series of sacral functions that were mostly related to religious ceremonies.

Khazar heavy cavalryman wearing full set of chainmail. (*Photo and copyright by Skjaldborg Vikings*)

Khazar heavy cavalryman wearing pointed helmet with an attached piece of chainmail. (*Photo and copyright by Skjaldborg Vikings*)

Khazar armoured horse archer. (*Photo and copyright by Skjaldborg Vikings*)

Khazarian society was dominated by warlike aristocrats, each of whom commanded a distinct military contingent and had a personal retinue of professional warriors. The Khazarian nobles grew rich thanks to revenues that derived from taxing the transit of foreign products. They were at the head of a diversified economy whose activities were a combination of traditional pastoralism, extensive agriculture, fishing on the course of the Volga River and craft manufacture. The Khazars were also very active in slave-trading and constructed several major urban settlements, like that of Atil, which later acted as the multi-ethnic capital of the Khazarian Khaganate. Until the beginning of the eighth century, Khazarian forces mostly consisted of horsemen, who operated for the defence of their home territories from a well-organized network of fortifications that acted as military bases. The Khazarian horsemen, as usual for the nomadic peoples of the steppes, could be heavily armoured cavalry or lightly equipped horse archers. The heavy cavalry were tasked with deciding the outcome of major pitched battles with their devastating charges, while the mounted archers performed a variety of auxiliary functions and had great tactical flexibility. The heavy cavalry, equipped with full armour, came from the aristocracy of Khazarian society and consisted of the nobles' retinues of professional warriors. The horse archers, instead, were made up of the ordinary Khazarian tribesmen. The Tarkhans, or noble warriors, also provided an elite bodyguard for their supreme rulers, which probably numbered around 1,000 heavy cavalrymen. The professional soldiers of the heavy cavalry were on permanent service and were paid regularly by the aristocrats who commanded them. However, the tribal horse archers were usually mobilized only in the case of war. By the middle of the tenth century, most of the Khazars lived in or around the mercantile city of Atil and were no longer nomadic, instead engaging in agriculture and trade on a permanent basis. As a result of this, military duties started to be partly transferred to subject peoples and mercenaries. Several Slavic tribes as well as the Alans were vassals of the Khazars, and as such they had to provide auxiliary military contingents, which were mostly tasked with guarding the frontiers of the Khazarian Khaganate. The foreign mercenaries were in most cases Muslim professional warriors who were recruited in large numbers by the Khazarian elites. According to some contemporary sources, these Muslim mercenaries were over time structured as a permanent military unit known as the Khwarazmian Guard, whose members settled permanently around the city of Atil. The Alan military organization was very similar to that of the Khazars, except for the fact that almost the entire Alan cavalry consisted of horse archers rather than heavily armoured cavalrymen. After settling permanently on the Caucasian territory of Alania, the Alans also started to deploy significant infantry contingents armed with wooden bows or axes.

Khazar pointed helmet. (*Photo and copyright by Skjaldborg Vikings*)

Khazar light cavalryman equipped with sabre and round shield.
(*Photo and copyright by Skjaldborg Vikings*)

Khazar horse archer; note the complexity of the decorative embroidering.
(*Photo and copyright by Skjaldborg Vikings*)

Khazar horse
archer. (*Photo and
copyright by
Skjaldborg Vikings*)

The standard Khazarian warrior's helmet was made of four iron segments riveted together, with a conical top element or finial and a straight nasal bar. Helmets often had a mail aventail attached to their rim, which reached the shoulders and was designed to protect the neck. Alan helmets were of the spangenhelm type and were often made of hardened leather elements attached to an iron frame (the latter consisting of a lower rim, eight vertical strips and a top plate). Khazarian armour comprised both chainmail and corselets of scale armour, which were frequently used in combination. The mail shirts were quite short in comparison with those produced in Western Europe and were short-sleeved. The corselets of scale armour could have their *lamellae* made from iron or leather. In most cases, a Khazarian heavy cavalryman wore a corselet of iron scale armour over a short mail shirt, which over time became long-sleeved and started to have slits in the hem of its skirt in order to prevent it from riding up when astride a horse. The Khazars produced some excellent corselets of scale armour, developing a system of loose riveting that required huge skill to be effective. This was as flexible as traditional scale construction but also considerably stronger, it being much more difficult to break its iron rivets than it was to cut the traditional lacing made with leather or rawhide. Late Khazarian armour also comprised domed shoulder plates forged from a single piece of steel and greaves forged from two substantial strips of metal that were connected by loops of rawhide or leather. The greaves were secured to the wearer's shins by buckled straps. The Khazars used the standard Turkic shield, which was round and approximately 78cm in diameter. This was made of five wooden boards that were connected to a crossbar, and was designed for protection against enemy arrows rather than for hand-to-hand combat. Khazarian composite bows were quite similar to the Hunnic ones, having ears consisting of elongated tapering plates with a notch for the bowstring. The shape of Khazarian bows gradually evolved, becoming more elongated and with the bowstring notch moving off-centre. The number of bone plates applied on each bow was reduced, together with the weight of the arrows. A standard Khazarian bowstring had loops to fit over the tips of the stave, which made it easier to replace a worn or damaged string. The Khazarian quivers were of the same kind employed by the Bulgars. Each Khazarian warrior, whether a heavy cavalryman or horse archer, was armed with a single-edged sabre that had a curved blade. This weapon often had a hilt that curved towards the cutting edge, and the length of its blade could vary greatly. Curvature of the sword was either uniform along the entire length of the blade or could be present only in the blade's final third. The point of the Khazarian sabres was double-edged, while the blade thickened towards the end in order to have greater striking power. The Khazars also used a Turkic fighting knife, which had a grip that markedly curved towards the cutting edge. This weapon was extremely effective

Alan light cavalryman.
(*Photo and copyright by Skjaldborg Vikings*)

Alan light cavalryman armed with nomadic form of flail. (*Photo and copyright by Skjaldborg Vikings*)

Alan light cavalryman.
(*Photo and copyright by Skjaldborg Vikings*)

Alan horse archer. (*Photo and copyright by Skjaldborg Vikings*)

Alan horse archer. (*Photo and copyright by Skjaldborg Vikings*)

for close combat. Spears were designed for their armour-piercing capacity and thus had tetrahedral heads that were mounted on slender wooden shafts, 3–4 metres long and made from straight saplings or pollard-poles of young trees. Saplings were cut in late autumn or early winter during the period of minimum sap flow; they were then straightened and allowed to dry, after which their wood was scraped and polished to obtain the desired size and shape. All the Alan light horsemen usually carried an effective battleaxe as a secondary weapon, which was later also adopted by the Khazarian heavy cavalrymen. This axe had a narrow elongated blade and could also have a secondary blade on the back of the head. War-flails were a popular alternative to the battleaxe: they were a type of mace consisting of a ball or other weight hanging from a short handle by means of a strap or plaited thongs. Like several other nomadic peoples, the Khazars used wood-framed saddles. Both Khazarian and Alan caps and tunics were quite similar to those worn by the Magyars and the Bulgars.

Chapter 7

The Turks, 552–1194

The Turkic people, or Turks, were one of the most important and powerful nomadic peoples of the Middle Ages. Following the migrations of the Huns, they gradually expanded across the vast plains of Central Asia. During the central decades of the sixth century, after having lived in a state of tribal anarchy, the Turks finally created a first form of unified state that became known as the First Turkic Khaganate. The Khaganate's main enemy, from the outset, were the White Huns. The Turks allied themselves with the Sasanian Empire ruled by Khosrow I in order to obtain a decisive victory over the Huns of Asia. In 557, at the Battle of Bukhara, the powerful alliance comprising Turks and Sasanians defeated the White Huns. The Huns never recovered from this clash, their empire soon fragmenting into several semi-independent principalities that had little military power. These principalities paid tribute to the Sasanians or the Turks, so were not fully independent. The Sasanians and the Turks established a frontier for their zones of influence in Central Asia along the Oxus River, with the White Huns' principalities functioning as buffer states between the two large empires. After the death of Khosrow I in 579, the White Huns revolted against the Sasanians, but their rebellion was soon crushed by the Turks, who were the new overlords of the nomadic peoples living in Central Asia. In 588, after having collaborated with the Sasanians for several decades, the Turks decided to invade Sasanian lands by crossing the Oxus River. The White Huns joined forces with the Turks and invaded a significant portion of the Sasanian territories, but were eventually repelled by the bulk of the enemy forces. The decades following these events saw a progressive decay of the Sasanian Empire, which had to wage war on several fronts against multiple enemies. In 606, there was a new war between Sasanians and Turks, which saw the participation of the Huns on the Turkic side. The nomads again obtained some initial victories until the Sasanians could mobilize their full military potential. Around 625, the eastern principalities of the White Huns permanently lost what remained of their political freedom, being annexed by the ever-expanding Turkic peoples. By the end of the seventh century, the Turks had created an immense empire in the steppes that extended from Manchuria in the east to the Caucasus in the west.

Turkish (Seljuk)
heavy cavalryman
equipped with spear
and round shield.
(*Photo and copyright by
Les Seigneurs d'Orient*)

Turkish (Seljuk) heavy cavalryman wearing corselet of lamellar armour. (*Photo and copyright by Les Seigneurs d'Orient*)

After coming into contact with the Arabs, who had conquered the Sasanian Empire during the early part of the seventh century, the Turkic peoples converted to Islam and gradually started to settle on the territories of present-day Iran. Thanks to their superior military capabilities, the Turkic warriors soon began to be employed as mercenaries by many Muslim rulers of the Middle East. The fighting methods employed by the Turks were extremely effective for the Arabs, so increasing numbers of nomadic warriors became part of the Muslim states' armies. During the early decades of the eleventh century, one section of the Turks – the mighty Seljuks – started migrating westwards from their homeland in Central Asia. By taking advantage of the regional rivalries that divided the various Arab states, the Seljuk Turks rapidly conquered the whole of present-day Iran and entered the Middle East. Within just a few years, they defeated on several occasions the Arab forces that tried to stop their expansion, meaning they could occupy vast areas of the Levant (including Syria and Palestine). The Seljuks, after defeating the Arab Caliphate of the Abbasids, conquered Mesopotamia and the flourishing Abbasid capital of Baghdad. They deployed massive cavalry armies of skilled horse archers, who were all equipped with the powerful composite bow of the Eurasian steppes, which gave them a marked military superiority over their Arab opponents. After having become the ruling power of the Muslim Levant, the Turks began attacking Byzantine territories in Anatolia in 1067. For some time, Byzantine armies were able to repel the offensives of the Seljuks, but the Turks were determined to conquer Anatolia for themselves. On 26 August 1071, a major pitched battle was fought between the Byzantines and the Turks at Manzikert in eastern Anatolia. The Byzantine troops, commanded by Emperor Romanos IV, consisted of 20,000 men (including large numbers of Norman mercenaries), whereas the Seljuk army of 30,000 horse arches was led by the expert commander Alp Arslan. During the battle, the Turks employed their elusive light cavalry tactics with great success and inflicted severe losses on the Byzantine forces, who were completely routed and could not prevent the capture of Romanos IV by the Seljuks.

After their brilliant victory, the Turks occupied the whole of Anatolia and almost caused the total collapse of the Byzantine Empire, which had been greatly weakened by the loss of its rich Anatolian provinces. In 1091, the Turks even besieged the imperial capital of Constantinople, but they were swiftly repulsed by the Byzantines. In 1092, Malik-Shah, the powerful warlord who had guided the Seljuks during the victorious campaigns of the previous years, died. This led to the outbreak of several bloody civil conflicts within the Turkic territories of the Middle East, which ended with their political fragmentation. The Anatolian territories of the Turks were organized as the Sultanate of Rum, while the Syrian lands now made up a separate state. In 1095, the Syrian state was divided into two rival emirates, one centred around Aleppo and the other on Damascus. As a result of the events outlined above, when the crusaders invaded the Middle East in 1096, they found the Muslims of the region divided among various rival states: the Seljuk Sultanate of Rum in Anatolia, the Seljuk Emirate of Aleppo in northern Syria, the Seljuk Emirate of Damascus in southern Syria, the Abbasid Caliphate in Iraq (what remained of it) and the Arab Fatimid Caliphate in Egypt. In March 1095, at Piacenza, a council took place of ecclesiastics and laymen of the Roman Catholic Church. During this meeting, Pope Urban II held talks with ambassadors sent by the Byzantine Emperor Alexius I Comnenus, who described to the synodal assembly the situation in which their state now found itself. The Byzantine envoys explained to the representatives of the Western Church how the Seljuks were in the process of invading the southern Balkans from Anatolia, menacing the imperial city of Constantinople. It was feared that the arrival of the Turks would be accompanied by massacres of Christian civilians, as had already happened in Anatolia after the Battle of Manzikert. Due to their military weakness, caused by the long wars fought against both the Fatimids and the Normans of southern Italy, the Byzantines were in no condition to organize an effective resistance against the Seljuks. Consequently, Alexius I had no alternative but to ask for help in Western Europe, where he hoped that the Christian leaders would decide to assist him by sending some troops.

After receiving full details of the difficult situation facing the Byzantine Empire, the pope decided to organize a new council in France during which he would ask the aristocracy to assemble a military expedition for the defence of Byzantine lands. This council took place at Clermont, in central France, in November 1097. The Kingdom of France was at this time the country of medieval Western Europe with the highest number of warlike nobles and knights. These, especially during the eleventh century, spent most of their time fighting against each other and thus had a very violent lifestyle. Urban II knew full well that the warlike feudal warlords represented a great military resource for the Christian world, since they were skilled warriors who loved fighting. The Pope felt that all the French aristocrats needed was a just and holy cause for which to campaign, possibly far away from their homelands that had already been devastated by too many feudal wars. Religious zeal was strong among the French knights, most of whom were true believers. Indeed, many of them feared that their violent lifestyle could have led their souls to damnation after death, and were consequently searching for a way to purify themselves of their many sins. At Clermont, in front of the most important aristocrats of France, Urban II proclaimed the Truce of God, an official decree by the Church that prohibited fighting among feudal lords for a specific period of time. After doing this, the pope invited the

Turkish (Seljuk) armoured horse archer. (*Photo and copyright by Les Seigneurs d'Orient*)

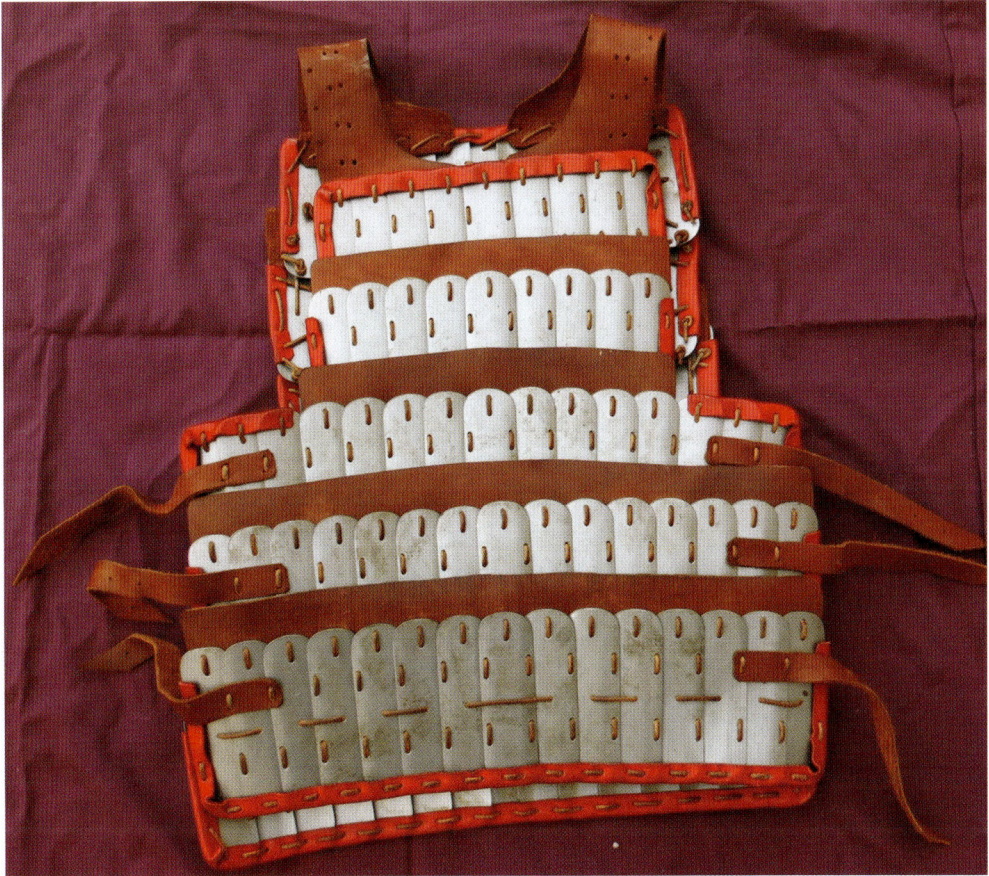

Turkish (Seljuk) corselet of lamellar armour.
(*Photo and copyright by Les Seigneurs d'Orient*)

warlike nobles to turn their attentions and energies away from feudal conflicts in order to defend the survival of the Christian faith in the eastern Mediterranean. He described how the Seljuk Turks had invaded Byzantine Anatolia and reached the Mediterranean, becoming a severe threat to the Christian world. These nomads of the steppes had killed or enslaved thousands of Christian people, devastating religious sites and slaughtering many members of the clergy. Having impressed his audience with his powerful words, Urban II issued a call to arms: all Christian people of whatever social condition – nobles or commoners – were asked to go to the aid of their Christian brothers in the Byzantine Empire.

The ensuing conflict was to be, according to the pope's words, a 'holy war': its main objective not being simply to defend the Byzantine Empire but to retake the Byzantine lands conquered by the Muslims during the previous centuries. The response of the nobles who were present at Clermont to Urban II's call to arms was spontaneous and enthusiastic: it was said that they cried '*Deus vult*' ('God wills it') in front of the pope, expressing their will to leave their homeland for the glory of religion. They soon became known as crusaders, from the Latin words *cruce signati* ('bearers of the cross'), since they started to wear crosses on their clothing and armour as a mark of distinction. Urban II hoped that the knights and peasants would fight together against the common enemy represented by the Muslims by forming a single Christian army that would head for Constantinople. However, this did not happen since two separate expeditions were organized. One, conducted by commoners, was known as the People's Crusade, while the other, involving some of the most powerful aristocrats of Western Europe, became known as the Princes' Crusade. The two expeditions were collectively known as the First Crusade. The People's Crusade was organized without the official permission of the Papacy by a charismatic monk and powerful orator named Peter the Hermit, who came from the French city of Amiens. Peter was well known in every corner of France for travelling around the countryside on a donkey and dressing in simple clothing. He was a true 'predicator', a poor monk who lived among the peasants and experienced their humble living conditions. Peter preached the crusade throughout northern France and Flanders, claiming to have been appointed to do so by Christ himself. The charismatic hermit eventually assembled a large number of peasants and low-ranking knights, who made up a giant band of illiterate pilgrims who had no idea of how to reach the Holy Land but still decided to launch a crusade of their own. Around 100,000 crusaders, including women and children, were under Peter's orders when the People's Crusade began in the summer of 1096. After having enlarged his army with many German commoners, Peter marched to the Danube, where his forces were split in two: some of them decided to continue by boat down the river, but most preferred continuing overland and entered Hungarian territory. In Zemun, not far from the border with the Byzantine Empire, a serious incident took place between the newly arrived crusaders and the local Hungarian population, which led to the storming of the city and the killing of more than 4,000 Hungarians (mostly civilians). The commoners then moved on Belgrade, which was evacuated by the Byzantines in order to avoid further massacres. The city was pillaged and burned by the crusaders, who continued their march across Byzantine territory.

The armed pilgrims from Western Europe behaved more violently and destructively than an invading army, raiding the countryside in search of supplies and killing everyone who tried to stop them. The Byzantine military authorities were forced to intervene to restore order and attacked the crusades, killing almost 10,000 of them. After this clash, the remaining 30,000 armed pilgrims were escorted by the Byzantine troops to Constantinople. Alexius I had no idea how to employ this

Turkish (Seljuk) warrior wearing helmet decorated with Islamic inscriptions. (*Photo and copyright by Les Seigneurs d'Orient*)

army of peasants that had reached his lands, fearing – correctly – that Peter's men could cause more devastations to his territory. As a result, he quickly ferried the crusades across the Bosporus and landed them on the Anatolian coastline. Knowing that most of them had no military capabilities to speak of, he hoped that the Seljuks would soon slaughter them. Once in Anatolia, the commoners began pillaging all the settlements that they encountered until they reached Nicomedia. Here, Peter the Hermit completely lost control of his army, with two new leaders being elected by the crusaders: one for the French and another for the Germans. The German commoners, numbering around 6,000, marched on Xerigordos and captured the fortress there. However, they were soon besieged in their newly conquered stronghold by the Seljuks. The outcome of the siege was decided by the lack of water among the crusaders, who after surrendering were all captured or enslaved by the Turks. The main crusader army, now consisting of approximately 20,000 French, built a large camp not far from Nicaea, where women and children could rest while the armed men patrolled the surrounding countryside in search of supplies. Three miles from the camp, along a road that entered a narrow and wooded valley, the Seljuks assembled a large cavalry army consisting of mounted archers. These ambushed the crusaders, massacring them in just a few minutes with a rain of deadly arrows.

Whereas the People's Crusade was little more than a disorganized mass pilgrimage, the Princes' Crusade was a well-planned military expedition. Under the direction of the Papacy, it started in August 1096 and consisted of four distinct armies that took different routes to Constantinople. According to modern estimates, around 100,000 individuals participated in the Princes' Crusade: 7,000 knights, 35,000 foot soldiers (mostly feudal peasant levies) and 60,000 civilian non-combatants (including women and children). The spiritual leader of the expedition was Adhemar of Le Puy, one of the most important French bishops, who had been chosen by the pope because of his military competence and great experience. There were many military leaders of the crusade, most of them coming from the dominant aristocratic families of France: Raymond IV of Toulouse, Godfrey of Bouillon, Baldwin of Boulogne, Hugh of Vermandois, Stephen II of Blois, Robert II of Flanders and Robert Curthouse. Raymond IV, Count of Toulouse, was the most powerful noble of southern France, while Godfrey of Bouillon, Duke of Lower Lorraine, was one of France's most experienced military commanders. Baldwin of Boulogne, Count of Verdun, was Godfrey of Bouillon's younger brother; Hugh of Vermandois, Count of Vermandois, was the younger brother of the King of France Philip I; and Stephen II of Blois, Count of Blois and Chartres, was one of the most powerful aristocrats of northern France and had married William the Conqueror's daughter, Adela of Normandy. Robert II, Count of Flanders, controlled one of Europe's richest regions located between France and Germany, while Robert Curthouse, Duke of Normandy, was the eldest son of William the Conqueror and the older brother of the King of England, William II. In addition to these leaders, there were two from southern Italy: Bohemond of Taranto and Tancred of Hauteville. Bohemond was the son of Robert Guiscard (the leader of the Norman adventurers who had conquered southern Italy) and was the Prince of Taranto; Tancred was a nephew of Bohemond and an ambitious young leader. The four crusader armies all headed for Constantinople, where they expected provisions from Alexius I. The emperor, in return for food and supplies, asked the western nobles to swear fealty to him and promise to return to the Byzantine Empire any land recovered from the Seljuks. Thereafter, the crusaders were ferried across the Bosporus by Byzantine naval forces.

After entering Turkic territory, the crusaders marched across Anatolia without encountering serious opposition. Their first target was the city of Nicaea, the capital of the Seljuk Sultanate of Rum. The Seljuks had already defeated the People's Crusade and did not expect the arrival of another European expedition. Their monarch, Arslan, was campaigning against a local enemy in central Anatolia and was not available to stop the advance of the crusaders. The western knights besieged Nicaea with all their forces, intending to seize the city in order to transform it into their main logistical base in Anatolia. Arslan, after having been informed of the threat to his capital, assembled all the forces that were at his disposal and advanced towards Nicaea. On 16 May 1097, the Turkic relief force attacked the crusaders, but was defeated during a bloody night battle. Both sides suffered severe losses, but the Seljuk army had no choice but to leave Nicaea to its destiny. Following this clash, some Byzantine troops joined the besieging crusaders. Alexius I feared that the westerners would keep Nicaea for themselves after taking it. Following the arrival of the Byzantine soldiers, being in a desperate situation, the defenders of Nicaea decided to surrender. However, they gave up the city to the overall commander of the Byzantine troops and not to any of the crusader leaders. Many of the crusaders were unhappy at this, as the Byzantines forbade them from entering Nicaea in groups larger than ten men at a time. Tension started to grow between the crusaders and the Byzantines, especially with the former having suffered significant losses in seizing the city. Alexius I gave the crusaders money and rich gifts, hoping that this would be enough to placate their indignation. Nicaea fell on 18 June 1097; eight days later, the crusaders left to continue their liberation of the Middle East from Muslim rule.

The western knights resumed their march in two contingents: one, comprising some Byzantine troops, was commanded by Bohemond and formed the vanguard; the other, including the best French troops, was under the orders of Godfrey and acted as the rearguard. While they reorganized themselves after the conquest of Nicaea, Arslan

Turkish (Seljuk) light cavalryman.
(*Photo and copyright by Les Seigneurs d'Orient*)

gathered a new and much larger army from his Seljuks. He then started to closely follow the movements of the crusaders' vanguard, awaiting the right opportunity to launch an ambush. On 1 July 1097, outside the settlement of Dorylaeum, Bohemond's Norman and Byzantine troops were surrounded by the Turks. Arslan launched a surprise attack while Bohemond's men were in their newly constructed camp. The crusader leaders had agreed that upon reaching Dorylaeum, their vanguard would halt and waited for the arrival of the reargrard. Initially, Bohemond's Normans suffered significant casualties, coming under a rain of arrows, but they soon recovered, mounted their horses and began to launch their own counter-attacks against the fast-moving Seljuk horse archers. The mounted bowmen, however, were much faster than the heavily armoured western knights and could not be caught by them. The Turks then rode into the enemy camp, cutting down large numbers of non-combatants and foot soldiers, who were unable to deploy in battle formation. At this point of the clash, to protect his infantry and civilians, Bohemond ordered his knights to dismount and form a defensive line. The foot soldiers and the non-combatants were gathered into the centre of the camp, where they tried to support the *milites* (knights). The Seljuks attacked the crusaders' defensive positions in their traditional style, charging in and shooting volleys of arrows before quickly retreating. Being on foot, the Norman knights could no longer mount effective counter-attacks and were instead obliged to play a passive tactical role. The Turkic arrows caused little harm to the armoured *milites*, but inflicted serious casualties to their horses, which were being kept in the centre of the defensive formation. Finding himself in an increasingly difficult situation, Bohemond sent messengers to the reargrard commanded by Godfrey and tried to resist for as long as possible. He was forced back to the banks of the Thymbris River, where the marshy terrain obliged the Seljuks to slow down their assaults. The knights formed a circle around the foot soldiers and civilians, but small groups of them occasionally broke ranks and charged the enemy, only to be slaughtered by the Turks. Despite being surprised by the ability of their opponents' armour to withstand the hail of arrows, the Turks controlled the battlefield and could move across it unimpeded because the crusaders had no missile troops to respond to the Seljuk archers. Just after midday, with the Bohemond's position started to become desperate, small groups of Godfrey's reinforcements began to reach the battlefield. After seven hours of fighting, Raymond IV arrived with a substantial number of *milites* and launched a surprise charge against one of the Seljuks' exposed flanks. This allowed the dispersed crusaders to rally and form a well-organized line of battle. The line of knights was rapidly deployed on the field in an offensive formation and launched a mass charge against the Turks in which all the most prominent crusader leaders participated. The Seljuks were surprised by the violence and power of their enemies' charge, having never

Turkish (Seljuk) heavy infantryman.
(*Photo and copyrigh by Les Seigneurs d'Orient*)

before seen feudal cavalry in action. Hundreds of unarmoured Turkic horse archers were slaughtered, particularly when further western reinforcements under Adhemar of Le Puy arrived on the battlefield and invested the Seljuk camp. Finding themselves surrounded and having no remaining hope of victory, the Turks started to flee. The Battle of Dorylaeum, against all the odds, ended in victory for the crusaders. Soon after the end of the battle, the crusaders looted the enemy camp and captured the rich treasury of Arslan. The Seljuk ruler, being in no condition to fight another battle against the invading *milites*, burned and destroyed everything he left behind in his army's flight, employing effective scorched earth tactics since it was the middle of summer and the crusaders had very few supplies with them in Anatolia. The local population of the region, who did not see the crusaders as liberators, did not help them by providing supplies. The crusader army was extremely numerous and needed huge amounts of water and food to continue their campaign. But with southern Anatolia not being particularly rich in such supplies, it proved a very inhospitable land for an invading force.

After passing through the Cilician Gates, the main crusader

army marched on to Antioch, one of the Middle East's most important and richest cities, situated midway between Constantinople and Jerusalem. Well-fortified and having a large population, it had to be taken by the crusaders if they wanted to continue their march across Syria. Upon reaching Antioch, the crusader leaders saw that it would be impossible for them to storm the city since its defences were too strong, so they started siege operations in the hope of forcing it to capitulate without having to suffer large losses. The siege began on 20 October 1097 and the crusaders quickly started to experience serious difficulties. First of all, they did not have enough troops to fully surround the city, so it was able to stay partially supplied. The army besieged Antioch for eight months without achieving anything; thousands of crusaders died of starvation, the supplies available to them being insufficient to sustain such a large force operating in a foreign country. Meanwhile, the Seljuk rulers of Aleppo and Damascus – two brothers who were waging war against each other – sent separate relief armies against the crusaders, both of which were easily defeated. Realizing that the western knights were too weak to conquer Antioch, the Turks decided to put aside their political differences and to raise a single relief army under the command of a leader named Kerbogha. Meanwhile, the leading crusader *milites* besieging Antioch spent much of the time quarrelling among themselves, each of them planning to transform the city into one of his personal domains. Bohemond, in particular, was determined to gain control of Antioch as it was the gateway to Syria. Stephen of Blois left the crusader army during the height of the siege and informed Alexius I that the Byzantine cause in the Middle East was lost, since the other crusader leaders had no intention to free any land for the Byzantines. Alexius I had assembled an army to support the western knights in their siege of Antioch and was marching through Anatolia when he was informed by Stephen about the real intentions of the crusader leaders. Now wishing the crusaders to be defeated by the Seljuks, the Byzantine emperor returned to his capital without sending any reinforcements or supplies to the western army. On 2 June 1097, however, an Armenian traitor living inside Antioch, having been paid by Bohemond, opened a gate of the city and helped a small party of crusader knights to enter. Seeing this, the Christian inhabitants of Antioch opened the other gates of their city in order to help the crusaders. After months of suffering virtual starvation, the besieging crusader forces acted with extreme violence after penetrating into the city. They sacked and killed with no mercy, causing significant loss of life, even among the Christian civilians of Antioch. The citadel of the city, however, remained in Turkic hands and continued to resist thanks to its strong fortifications.

On 4 June 1097, the vanguards of Kerbogha's army of 40,000 men finally arrived outside Antioch. The crusaders, taken by surprise, had little time to improvise

Turkish (Seljuk) sword. (*Photo and copyright by Les Seigneurs d'Orient*)

a defence of the city they had only just captured. Fortunately for them, though, Antioch's walls had not been seriously damaged during the lengthy siege operations. From 10 June 1097, for four days, Kerbogha's troops assaulted Antioch's walls from dawn until dusk. The crusaders, despite being heavily outnumbered, managed to hold out. The city gates were barred to prevent desertions and the civilian population was forced to support the crusaders in every way they could. Having been repulsed several times, the Turks halted their assaults and settled down to besiege the city in the hope of starving the crusaders into surrender. Morale inside Antioch soon plummeted, especially when hundreds of soldiers and civilians started to die of starvation. Once again, the crusaders did not have enough supplies with them and had failed to effectively plan the logistical aspect of their military actions. When everything seemed lost, a peasant visionary who was with the crusader army – named Peter Bartholomew – claimed that Saint Andrew had shown him the location of the Holy Lance that had pierced Christ on the cross. The Holy Lance was found exactly where Peter Bartholomew searched for it, and this boosted the morale of the exhausted defenders. Having by now run out of supplies but being full of religious zeal, the crusaders marched out of Antioch in four groups on 28 June 1097 to engage the enemy in a decisive – albeit desperate – pitched battle. Kerbogha did not try to stop the deployment of the enemy army, as he wanted to destroy the crusaders as quickly as possible and was confident of his soldiers' superiority. Kerbogha's troops, however, did not consist only of Seljuks, also comprising large numbers of non-professional fighters. Consequently, when the crusaders deployed out of Antioch, the Muslims launched a disorderly attack against them. The crusaders, knowing that their destiny depended on the battle, charged headlong into the Muslim army with violent desperation and quickly killed hundreds of them. The besieging army of Kerbogha was completely destroyed, the survivors being forced to withdraw from the region. Following the success of the western knights, the defenders of the city's citadel decided to surrender. It had been a complete victory for the crusaders, and especially for Bohemond, who thereafter became the ruler of Antioch.

Bohemond soon argued that Alexius I's decision to abandon the crusaders to their destiny had invalidated all their oaths to him, so following the conquest of Antioch they began to act independently from the Byzantines and the whole crusade assumed a new nature. They were now fighting to conquer the Holy Land for themselves, not to restore the Byzantine presence in the Middle East. After occupying Antioch, the crusaders again began quarrelling between themselves and remained passive for several months. Now that the expedition had turned itself into a campaign of conquest, all the various leaders wanted to create their own states in the Middle East. While they discussed how best to continue the campaign, a plague broke out among the ranks of the crusader army and killed many hundreds, including Adhemar, who had tried to limit the ambitions of the various warlords and to keep the crusade under the direct control of the pope. The crusader forces were in no condition to continue their march across the Middle East, having halted at Antioch for so many months; they now had very few horses and suffered from a chronic lack of supplies. The Muslim peasants living in the countryside around Antioch refused to give them food, and all the nearby areas had already been pillaged during the previous months. Once again being on the verge of starvation, the crusaders had no choice but to restart their advance towards the heartland of the Holy Land in early 1099. They encountered little resistance during this phase of their expedition, the local rulers of the area between northern Syria and Palestine preferring to make peace with them and to furnish them with supplies rather than seeing their lands devastated. The successes of the crusaders caused the rapid collapse of the Seljuk military presence in the Levant, aided by the Fatimids having taken advantage of the Turks' difficulties to invade Palestine from Egypt. A few months before the arrival of the western knights

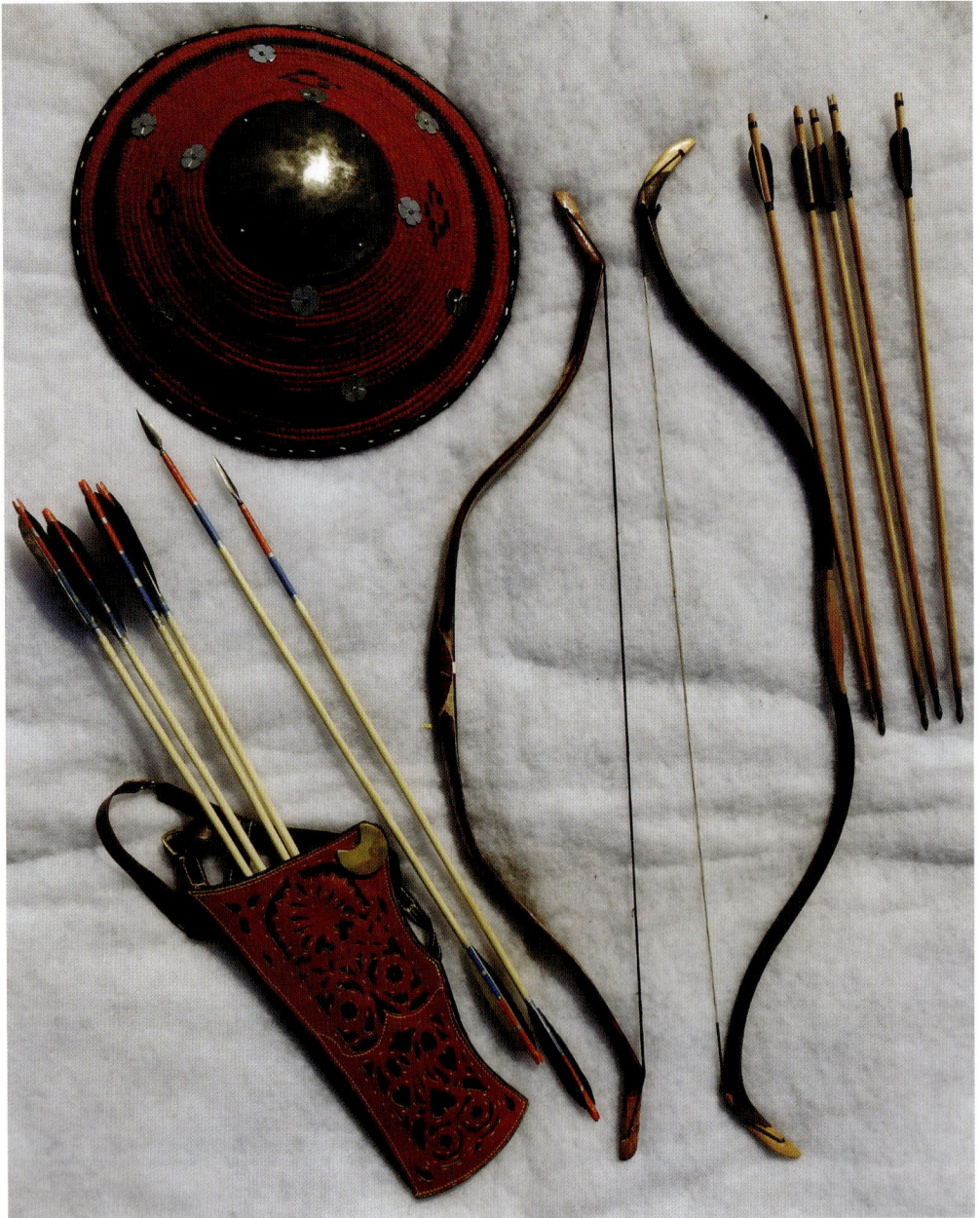

The personal panoply of a Turkish (Seljuk) warrior, including two composite bows and a quiver with arrows as well as a small round shield. (*Photo by Attila Kiss and Tömör, copyright by Kőmíves Nelli Admira*)

in front of its walls, the Holy City of Jerusalem was occupied by the Fatimids, who expelled the Seljuks. Following the crusaders' conquest of Jerusalem and the end of the First Crusade in 1099, the Turks' domains in the Middle East fragmented into a series of minor states that had little political importance or military capability. These states had all disappeared by 1157, except for the Sultanate of Rum in Anatolia, which continued to exist until 1308, after which it fragmented into a series of minor Turkic states, including the early Ottoman one. By 1194, all the Seljuk territories in Iran and Central Asia had also lost their independence, to the advantage of a new Muslim state – the Khwarezmid Empire – that was later destroyed by Gengis Khan.

The society of the early Turks was structured on clans, each of which comprised a variable number of families. The various clans were themselves assembled into larger tribal groups, each of which was guided by a warlord known as a '*beg*'. The different tribes were led by a supreme military ruler called a '*khan*', which later became the Arab title of 'sultan' after the Seljuks conquered the Muslim Middle East. All able-bodied Turkic men were warriors and were expected to serve in times of war. According to contemporary written sources and to archaeological finds, the early Turkic cavalry armies consisted almost entirely of lightly equipped mounted archers, with only the noble warriors equipped as heavy cavalrymen. The standard Turkic horse archer was armed with a composite bow and curved sabre, so Turkic tactics were based on repeated archery attacks and feigned retreats. The Turks were also famous for being able to organize deadly ambushes. Daily life was extremely harsh for these nomads, who were used to enduring all kinds of hardships. They lived in heavy tents made of felt and their diet was based on milk and meat. Each Turkic man had at least ten horses, which were extremely well-trained and had incredible endurance. Once in battle, every Turkic horse archer always had a fresh mount at his disposal, enabling him to move much more rapidly than his enemies. While on campaign, each Turkic horse had a bag hung on his nose in which fodder was put, meaning that Turkic warriors could travel long distances with their horses by day or night without having to stop moving.

During the eleventh century, as a result of their conquest of the Middle East and their partial transformation into a sedentary people, the Seljuk Turks had to modify their traditional military organization. The Seljuk armies started to comprise two main categories of troops: those belonging to the central army of the sultan and those under the orders of the provincial military commanders, or '*amirs*'. Members of the Seljuk central army were known as '*askars*' and were a full-time professional force that was paid in cash or according to the '*iqta*' system. This had a quasi-feudal nature, since it consisted of assigning grants of land to soldiers in exchange for their military service. The *iqta* could be a hereditary benefice, passing from father to son, or just a lifetime one. It was transferable from province to province, since unlike the feudal fiefs of Western Europe, it did not represent a personal estate but a payment in land revenues for the military services rendered. The *askars* who received the largest and richest land grants usually acted as amirs or provincial commanders;

Turkish (Seljuk) composite bow and leather quiver with arrows.
(*Photo by Attila Kiss and Tömör, copyright by Kőmíves Nelli Admira*)

these had to raise a specific number of fighters from the territories that were under their control, usually slave-soldiers who were bonded to their warlords for lifetime service or foreign auxiliaries who were recruited from the local communities that had been submitted by the Seljuks (such as the Kurds, who lived on mountainous terrain and provided warlike foot skirmishers). After establishing themselves in the Middle East, the Seljuk Turks started to include significant numbers of foot soldiers in their military forces. These were provided by the foreign auxiliaries mentioned above or by the '*ahdath*' ('urban militias') that existed in many of the cities which had been conquered by them. The slave-soldiers, or '*ghulams*', who made up the bulk of the provincial cavalry mostly came from the ethnic groups that had been submitted by the Seljuks: Daylamis, Khorasanians, Georgians and Turcomans. The latter were also known as Oghuz Turks, being those Turks who had remained in Central Asia (in the original homeland of their people) after the Seljuks migrated westwards to invade Iran. The Turcomans were wilder than the Seljuks and often terrorized the crusaders. As a result, the Seljuk sultans settled thousands of them on their territories in order to have sizeable numbers of Turcoman fighters at their disposal. The *ghulams* were purchased as slaves while they were still young males and grew up with the Turks, who trained them in the use of arms. A *ghulam* was instructed and educated at his master's expense and could earn his freedom through dedicated service. Over time, especially following the First Crusade, these slave-soldiers became the core of the Muslim armies of the Middle East because of their reliability. They also gradually replaced the *askars* in the central army of the Seljuk sultans and started to receive land grants according to the *iqta* system. Consequently, the Seljuk and Turcoman slave-soldiers were a fundamental component of Saladin's forces during the Third Crusade. The *ghulams* were the direct predecessors of the famous Mamluks of Egypt and the mighty Janissaries deployed by the Ottoman Turks. After the Mongols conquered the whole of Central Asia, thousands of nomadic warriors – mostly Cumans and

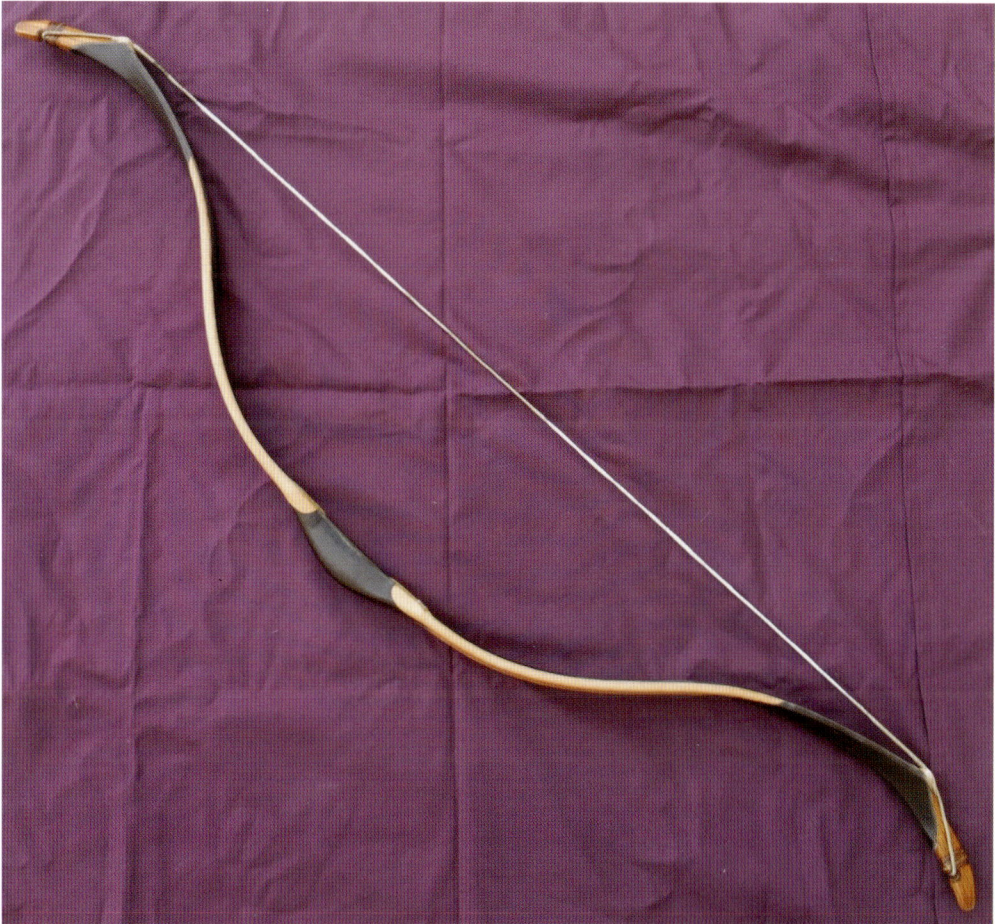

Turkish (Seljuk) composite bow. (*Photo and copyright by Les Seigneurs d'Orient*)

Kipchaks – migrated to the Middle East, where they offered their military services to the local Muslim states as *ghulams*.

Turkic clothes were made from sheepskin, generally including a pointed cap trimmed with fur and a knee-length tunic. The tunic was often trimmed with wool and was usually worn under a long topcoat. Turkic trousers were quite baggy and were worn tucked into comfortable leather boots that covered the whole knee. The Turkic composite bow was carried in a case, which was used together with a quiver that could store a significant number of arrows. Each Turkic warrior also had a sabre, which was single-edged and had a slightly curved blade. The few nobles wearing cuirasses usually had a corselet of scale or lamellar armour that was occasionally worn over a padded jacket of quilted armour (aketon) or with a camail of chainmail. Sometimes, two iron discs, fastened on leather straps, could be worn over the shoulders or on the chest for additional protection. Turkic helmets had a sphero-conical form and a rectangular cut-out above the face, which was sometimes covered by a face mask also serving as a protective visor. The Turks also had shields, which were oval in shape and quite small since they were designed for protecting their user from enemy arrows. Turkic horse equipment did not include any protective element, but comprised a wood-framed saddle. The Turks were famous for their short whips, which were employed to control the horses but also to strike enemies at close range.

Chapter 8

The Pechenegs, Cumans and Kipchaks, 850–1262

The Pechenegs originated as subjects of the Turkic Khaganate, their homeland being located between Lake Aral and the middle course of the Syr Darya River. Around AD 850, they were defeated in battle by the Turks near Lake Aral and were forced to abandon their homeland. They started to develop an autonomous culture soon after these events and migrated westwards. Along the way, the Pechenegs fought on several occasions against the Khazars, who defended their territories in the Caucasus and prevented the Pechenegs from settling in the region. After a long and difficult migration, the Pechenegs established themselves on the vast area located between the rivers Donets and Kuban. After developing their new homeland, they soon came under increasing pressure from other steppe peoples, most notably the Khazars and the Cumans, who considered them to be dangerous rivals. The Pecheneg lands were often raided by other nomadic peoples, who seized livestock and other goods during their bloody incursions. In order to stabilize their position in Eastern Europe, the Pechenegs established positive diplomatic relations with the Byzantine Empire and the Bulgars. In particular, they joined the Bulgars in their struggle against the Magyars. The Pechenegs, thanks to their superior combat skills, obtained a series of brilliant victories over the Magyars and expelled them permanently from the Pontic Steppe. After these events, they came to control most of present-day Ukraine, including Crimea, during the tenth century. The Pechenegs' 'golden age' came to an end with the military ascendancy of the Kievan Rus, which soon became their fiercest enemy. For several decades, the nomadic Pechenegs launched raids against the large state that had been created by the Eastern Vikings, even besieging Kiev during 968. Four years later, the Pechenegs ambushed and killed Svyatoslav I, the prince who had transformed Kievan Rus into the leading power of Eastern Europe. According to a contemporary source, the Pecheneg leader Kurya made a chalice from Svyatoslav's skull, as was an ancient tradition of the steppe peoples. With the progression of time, however, the Kievan Rus gained the upper hand in the confrontation with the Pechenegs. Indeed, by 1036 the Pechenegs had been defeated several times by the heirs of the Varangians. This greatly favoured the Cumans, who formed a strong alliance with the Byzantine Empire. In 1091, the Byzantines and the Cumans decisively defeated the Pechenegs at the Battle of Levounion, which halted any further

Cuman heavy
cavalryman wearing
corselet of leather
armour. (*Photo and
copyright by Iloncsuk
Szabadcsapat*)

Cuman heavy cavalryman wearing corselet of chainmail.
(*Photo and copyright by Iloncsuk Szabadcsapat*)

Cuman heavy cavalryman wearing pointed felt cap, which was also extremely popular among the Magyars. (*Photo and copyright by Iloncsuk Szabadcsapat*)

Pecheneg attempt to invade Byzantine lands and was followed by a massive Cuman invasion of Pecheneg territory during 1094. The few communities of Pechenegs who survived these events crossed the Danube during 1122 in a desperate attempt to invade the Byzantine Empire. However, they were annihilated at the Battle of Beroia, after which the remaining Pechenegs were either resettled on Byzantine lands as military colonists or established themselves in Hungary as vassals of the Christian kingdom created by the Magyars.

The Cumans and the Kipchaks were two nomadic peoples of Turkic stock that were strongly related to each other. They originated in the vast steppes located north-east of the Chinese Empire and – during their early history – fought a series of wars against each other. The sources available to reconstruct the historical origins of the Cumans and the Kipchaks are extremely scarce, but it is plausible to say that the Cumans prevailed over the Kipchaks and formed a single tribal confederation. This, starting from the late ninth century AD, spread its political influence across the Eurasian steppes and gradually came to control a vast territory that extended from the Altai Mountains in Mongolia to the Pontic Steppe in Ukraine. The Cumans settled on the western portion of this enormous area, while the Kipchaks dominated the eastern part. During the eleventh century, the destinies of the Cumans and the Kipchaks became separated, with the former migrating westwards in order to settle in Eastern Europe while the latter remained in Asia. The Cumans began their expansion in Eastern Europe when the region was already controlled by three significant military powers: the Byzantine Empire, the Kingdom of Hungary (established by the Magyars) and the Kievan Rus. The Cumans confronted the Kievan Rus for the first time in 1055, when they invaded and devastated a portion of Russian territory before being paid a tribute in exchange for stopping their incursions. Some years later, in 1061, they again attacked the Russian lands, this time on a larger scale. The Cumans took advantage of the political instability that had emerged within the Kievan Rus after the death of Yaroslav the Wise, the leader who had transformed the state created by the Varangians into a major power. In 1068, at the Battle of the Alta River, they defeated the joint military forces of Yaroslav the Wise's three sons. After this victory, the Cumans repeatedly invaded the territory of the Kievan Rus, devastating large areas and taking thousands of captives who were sold as slaves. They obtained another significant victory over the Russians at the Battle of the Stugna River in 1093, which was followed by four Cuman attacks against the city of Kiev. The Cumans, during the late eleventh century, also conducted a series of attacks against Hungary. In 1099, they crushed a Hungarian army in battle and seized the Hungarian royal treasury, which had a devastating impact on the finances of the Magyar realm. During those same years, the Cumans also fought against the Byzantine Empire and the Bulgars, devastating large swathes of the Balkanson several occasions. In some cases, the nomads formed temporary alliances with their enemies in order to achieve common objectives. As we have seen, for example, the Cumans temporarily allied themselves with the Byzantines to defeat the Pechenegs. Within a few years of their victory at the Battle of Levounion, the Cumans were able to eradicate the Pecheneg presence in modern Ukraine and to remain as the only nomadic power of Eastern Europe. Over the years, Cuman incursions became increasingly audacious, their raids even reaching the richest cities of Poland and Lithuania. No military power in Eastern Europe seemed capable of defeating the Cumans, who moved with great rapidity across vast areas and were capable of winning pitched battles against superior enemy forces. The Cumans also expanded into the Caucasus, where some of them achieved prominent positions within the Christian Kingdom of Georgia. The Cumans who settled in there helped the Georgians to halt the expansionism of the Muslim Seljuk Turks and transformed Georgia – albeit for only a short time – into a significant regional power.

By 1160, the Cuman raids into Kievan Rus had become an annual event and were starting to have terrible consequences for the Russian economy. The presence of the

Cuman heavy cavalryman armed with sabre and mace. (*Photo and copyright by Iloncsuk Szabadcsapat*)

Kipchak armoured horse archer; both the facial mask and the discs worn on the chest were distinctive of the Kipchaks and Cumans. (*Photo by Jasmin Parvanov, copyright by Equestrian Martial Arts School – Madara Horseman, Obzor, Bulgaria, and Association for Restoration and Preservation of Bulgarian Traditions – Avitohol, Varna, Bulgaria*)

of present-day Romania. While the Cumans played a prominent role on the military scene of Eastern Europe, the Kipchaks who had remained in Asia started migrating towards the Islamic world during the early eleventh century. The Kipchaks were not alone in this migration, with other nomadic peoples such as the Seljuk Turks also moving from the steppes of Central Asia into the rich territories of the Middle East. Both the Kipchaks and the Seljuks started to be employed in large numbers as mercenaries by the Muslim states of the Middle East, but the Kipchaks had less success than the Seljuks during this early phase since – differently from the latter – they were not capable of conquering any part of the Islamic world for themselves.

The rise of the Mongols under the leadership of Genghis Khan, which took place during the early decades of the thirteenth century, had enormous consequences for both the Cumans and the Kipchaks. After conquering Alania in the Caucasus, the Mongols attacked the Kipchaks and defeated them on several occasions. Within a few years, the vast territories that had been dominated by the Kipchaks were occupied by the Mongols, who were in the process of conquering the whole of Eurasia. The surviving Kipchaks fled to the Principality of Kiev, where they established a solid anti-Mongol alliance with the Russians. The Kipchaks were valuable allies for the Russian princes, their excellent light cavalry made up of horse archers having the same scouting and skirmishing capabilities as the Mongols. The Cumans were also badly affected by the sudden appearance of the Mongols. They were first attacked in the Caucasus by Mongol forces that had just destroyed the Muslim state of Khwarazam; being militarily inferior, the Cumans were defeated and forced to flee north. At this point, like the Kipchaks, they decided to join forces with the Russian princes and to become part of a large anti-Mongol alliance. After a meeting in Kiev between the Russian and the Cuman-Kipchak leaders, it was decided that the forces of the anti-Mongol alliance would move east in search of a decisive pitched battle against the invading Mongols. This clash took place in 1223 near the Kalka River and ended in a disastrous defeat for the anti-Mongol army. Thousands of Russians were killed during the battle, but the Cumans and Kipchaks were able to flee and save a good number of their troops. In 1236, after a few years of peace, the Mongols renewed their invasion of Eastern Europe, crossing the Volga River in great numbers. Their main objective was now to destroying the Cumans and Kipchaks, who still represented a formidable enemy (unlike the Russian princedoms, which were extremely weak from a military point of view). During 1238 and 1239, the Cuman lands in Eastern Europe came under direct Mongol attack. Although the Cumans and the Kipchaks defended their territory with great courage, by 1241 the Mongols had become the sole masters of the Pontic Steppe. The defeated Cumans and Kipchaks were left with no option but to migrate as refugees since they refused to be absorbed by the Mongols.

Kipchak heavy cavalryman equipped with sabre and small round shield. (*Photo and copyright by Iloncsuk Szabadcsapat*)

Kipchak heavy cavalryman wearing pointed felt cap. (*Photo and copyright by Iloncsuk Szabadcsapat*)

Around 40,000 Cuman families moved to the Kingdom of Hungary, where they were welcomed by King Bela IV, who permitted them to settle on the eastern borders of his realm. The nomads became part of the Hungarian forces and converted to Christianity, since Bela IV wanted to transform them into a precious military resource that could be employed during the upcoming Mongol invasion of Hungary. As for the Kipchaks, after being defeated they preferred to move across the southern Balkans and to migrate to the Muslim territories of the Middle East. Here, many of them converted to Islam and started to serve as mercenaries in the Muslim armies, especially in the ranks of the Mamluks who had ruled Egypt since 1250. The Kipchaks, together with other mercenaries who served in Egypt as slave-soldiers, were one of the founding elements of the Mamluks, who in 1260 soundly defeated the Mongols at the Battle of Ain Jalut. This put a definitive stop to Mongol expansion in the Middle East and was a triumph for the Mamluk Sultan Baibars, who had Kipchak origins. The Cumans who settled in the Kingdom of Hungary retained their distinct ethnic nature but soon started to cooperate with the local political authorities. The incursions of the Cumans had long represented a major military problem for the Hungarians, who had even granted one of their border regions to the Teutonic Knights during 1211 in the hope that they could effectively counter the nomadic incursions. Now that the Cumans were subjects of the Hungarian crown, it seemed that peace and order could be restored in the Hungarian frontier lands, but this never happened due to the outbreak of hostilities between the Kingdom of Hungary and the Mongols. The Mongols ordered Bela IV to stop giving refuge to the Cumans because they wanted to destroy once and for all a nomadic population that they still regarded as a potential obstacle to their expansion. In March 1241, the Mongols attacked the Hungarian defences at the Carpathian passes, initiating a massive invasion. They advanced very rapidly, defeating the Hungarians on several occasions and taking numerous important cities. The Hungarians made the mistake of not employing the Cumans in battle as they did not have complete trust in them. The Cumans, wishing to retain their independence from the Mongols, decided to leave Hungary before Bela IV was completely routed by the invaders. Luckily for the Hungarians, the Mongol invasion of 1241–1242 did not become a permanent occupation of their lands, being restricted to a large-scale raid with no enduring political consequences. After the Mongols left Hungary, Bela IV invited the Cumans to return to Hungary in order to repopulate the areas that had been devastated by the Asiatic invaders. The Cumans accepted and were settled on two regions of the Great Hungarian Plain that became known as Greater Cumania and Lesser Cumania. The Cumans were granted rights and privileges by the Hungarian monarch, who wanted to use them to limit the power of his unstable aristocracy. In 1262, the Cuman communities were placed under the direct control of the Hungarian monarchy, which initiated a long process of cultural integration that gradually led to the full absorption of the nomads into Hungarian society.

Politically, the Pechenegs always remained a loose association of clans that were assembled into large tribal groups. Differently from the Khazars, they never built fortifications and never settled down to practice commerce with other peoples. Their major source of income was through slave-trading, which made most of the Pecheneg aristocrats very rich. Unlike the Khazarian nobility, Pecheneg aristocrats did not have large personal retinues of professional warriors under their orders. Indeed, Pecheneg society was quite egalitarian, with all the able-bodied free men who were part of it enjoying the same rights and having the same military duties. Each Pecheneg man was a warrior and had to serve as a horse archer. According to Byzantine written sources and to archaeological finds, the Pecheneg cavalry armies consisted almost entirely of lightly equipped mounted archers, since only the few noble warriors were equipped as heavy cavalry. The Pecheneg horse archers are described as being clean-shaven and were dressed similarly to the Magyars. Their standard headgear was a pointed cap, which usually had earflaps and was trimmed with fur. The standard Pecheneg tunic was very similar to that worn by the Avars, being knee-length and loose fitting. It could have rich decorations on the external edges and was often trimmed with fur on the collar or around the cuffs. The tunics of the aristocrats could be made of silk and have complex embroidering. Over the tunic, especially during the colder months, Pecheneg warriors wore a long topcoat that had the same basic features as the tunic; this, in most cases, had side-vents since it was designed for riding. Pecheneg trousers were quite baggy and were worn tucked into comfortable boots made of leather. The Pecheneg composite bow had the same basic features as that used by the Avars, being extremely effective from medium distances. It was carried in a case, while a quiver for the arrows was very similar to that employed by the Huns. Each Pecheneg warrior also had a sabre, which was single-edged and had a slightly curved blade. A short dagger, which also had a curved blade, was usually carried in the waistbelt. The few nobles wearing cuirasses usually had a corselet of scale armour that was worn over a short-sleeved chainmail. Helmets were quite rare among the Pechenegs, being worn only by the aristocrats; they had a sphero-conical form and a rectangular cut-out above the face, which was in turn covered by a face mask serving as a protective visor. The face mask often had human-like decorations and could be made of bronze. Pecheneg horse equipment did not include any protective elements, but did include a wood-framed saddle very similar to that used by the Avars. The Pechenegs were famous for their ox-headed bugles, which were used to transmit orders on the battlefield over long distances. Pecheneg battle tactics were based on repeated archery attacks and feigned retreats.

The Cumans and the Kipchaks had the same social and military organization, so what is written here about the Cumans is perfectly valid for the Kipchaks as well. Cuman society was structured on clans, each of which comprised a variable number of families, with the clans forming larger tribal groups, each of which was under the orders of a warlord or *beg*. The various tribes, or hordes, were led by a supreme military ruler or *khan*. All able-bodied Cuman men were warriors and were expected to serve during times of war, and the Cuman women could also fight in case of need, exactly as did the Pecheneg women. According to contemporary written sources and archaeological finds, the Cuman cavalry armies consisted almost entirely of lightly equipped mounted archers, with only the noble warriors equipping themselves as heavy cavalrymen. The standard Cuman horse archer was armed with a composite bow, throwing javelins and curved sabre, with Cuman tactics based on repeated archery attacks and feigned retreats, just like the Pechenegs. The Cumans were also famed for their ability to organize ambuscades. Daily life was extremely harsh for these nomads, who were used to enduring all kinds of hardships. They lived in heavy tents made of felt and their diet was based on milk and meat. Each Cuman man had between ten and twelve horses, which were very resilient and extremely well-trained. When in

Kipchak heavy cavalryman. (*Photo and copyright by Iloncsuk Szabadcsapat*)

Cuman heavy
cavalryman from
the late thirteenth
century. (*Photo and
copyright by Iloncsuk
Szabadcsapat*)

Cuman heavy cavalryman from the late thirteenth century. (*Photo and copyright by Iloncsuk Szabadcsapat*)

battle, Cuman horse archers always had a fresh mount at their, which enabled them to move much more rapidly than their enemies. While on campaign, Cuman horses had bags of fodder hung on their noses, enabling Cuman warriors to cover vast distances without having to stop, both during the day and at night. Cuman clothes were very similar to those worn by the Pechenegs, being made from sheepskin and comprising a pointed cap trimmed with fur and a knee-length tunic. The tunic was often trimmed with wool and was usually worn under a long topcoat. Cuman trousers were baggy and worn tucked into leather boots. The Cuman composite bow had the same basic features as the Pecheneg one and was carried in a special case, while a quiver could store a significant number of arrows. Cuman warriors also fought with a sabre, which was single-edged with a slightly curved blade. The few nobles wearing cuirasses usually had a corselet of scale armour that was worn over a short-sleeved chainmail. Two iron discs, fastened on leather straps, could occasionally be worn over the chainmail on the shoulders or on the chest for additional protection. Cuman helmets had a sphero-conical form and a rectangular cut-out above the face, which was in turn covered by a face mask that acted as a protective visor. Differently from the Pechenegs, the Cumans also had shields. These were oval in shape and were quite small, being designed to protect their user from javelins, which were extremely common to find among the Cumans (who were famous for their accuracy in throwing them). The Cumans, like the Huns and other steppe peoples, could also employ lassos on the battlefield together with other secondary weapons designed for hand-to-hand combat, such as maces. The Cuman horse equipment included no protective element but comprised a wood-framed saddle very similar to that used by the Pechenegs. The Cumans were famous for their short whips, which were employed to control the horses but also to hit out at nearby enemies. Unlike several of the other nomadic peoples, the Cumans shaved their chins and wore their hair long.

Cuman noble warrior. (*Photo by Dimitar Atanassov, IEFSEM-BAS, Experiencing History Research Project, copyright by Kalina Atanasova, https://badamba. info/, Bulgaria, and Association for Restoration and Preservation of Bulgarian Traditions – Avitohol, Varna, Bulgaria*)

Cuman horse archer from the late thirteenth century.
(*Photo and copyright by Iloncsuk Szabadcsapat*)

Cuman horse archer from the late thirteenth century. (*Photo and copyright by Iloncsuk Szabadcsapat*)

Chapter 9

The Mongols of Genghis Khan, 1125–1227

From the mid-tenth century onwards, the vast steppes of present-day Mongolia and Manchuria were inhabited by five powerful tribal confederations: the Keraites, Khamags, Naimans, Mergids and Tatars. These large nomadic groups consisted of communities that had a lot of cultural elements in common, since they were all of Mongolian stock. Nevertheless, the five tribal groupings were almost continuously fighting against each other for control of the best pasture lands. The Mongol communities had an enormous military potential, since they were the strongest and wildest tribes among the peoples of the Eurasian steppes, but their lack of unity made them quite weak politically. This was used to their advantage by the Chinese, whose vast empire extended just south of the Mongol lands. In 1125, the northern area of China came under the control of a new imperial bloodline known as the Jin Dynasty, which continued the foreign policy of its predecessors regarding the Mongols that was based on the principle of divide and rule. The Chinese encouraged disputes among the Mongol tribal confederations in order to keep them distracted by their own internal wars and thereby away from Jin territories. In those years, the Khamags tried to unify the Mongol communities by forming a confederation, but this early attempt – carried out by Khabul Khan, the great-grandfather of Genghis Khan – failed completely due to the opposition of the Jin Dynasty. Khabul Khan's successor, Ambaghai Khan, was betrayed by the Tatars and handed over to the Jin authorities before being executed by them. The Khamags responded by raiding along the Chinese frontier and repulsing a Jin invasion of their homeland in 1143. It was during this chaotic period, characterized by several inter-nomadic wars, that the future Genghis Khan was born in 1162 with the initial name of Temujin. The years of his childhood saw the Khamags – the tribal confederation ruled by Temujin's family – fighting a series of conflicts against the Tatars and the Jin military forces. In 1161, a joint army of Tatar and Jin troops had defeated the Khamags in a significant battle, meaning it was not easy for Temujin's family to keep power during the central decades of the twelfth century. If the political situation of Mongolia was very negative during the years of Temujin's childhood, however, the same could not be said of the climatic one. Indeed, the late twelfth century saw the steppes of Mongolia enjoying their mildest and wettest conditions in more than a millennium. This favoured a rapid

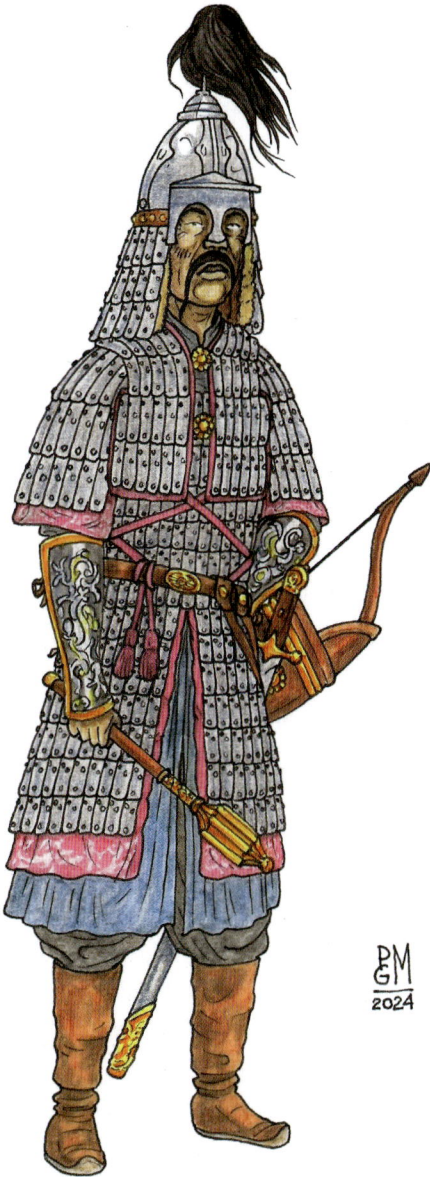

Mongol heavy cavalryman wearing full set of lamellar armour and armed with a mace. (*Colour plate by Patricio Greve Moller, copyright by Gabriele Esposito*)

Mongol heavy cavalryman wearing full set of lamellar armour and armed with a sabre. (*Colour plate by Patricio Greve Moller, copyright by Gabriele Esposito*)

increase in the number of horses and other livestock, which significantly enhanced Mongol military strength.

In 1177, Temujin initiated his incredible military ascendancy by gathering 20,000 warriors to attack the Mergids, who had kidnapped his wife during a raid. He had earlier formed a solid alliance with the Keraites, which was essential for the success of his expedition. After rescuing his wife, Temujin continued to fight against the Mergids for several years, co-operating with another young military leader of the Khamags, named Jamukha, who was his blood brother. At some point, however, the friendship between Temujin and Jamukha came to an end due to the contrasting interests of the two emerging leaders. In 1193, at the Battle of Dalan Baljut, Temujin and Jamukha fought for supremacy over the Khamag communities. Being outnumbered by his former allies, Temujin was defeated in the clash, but the encounter was not a decisive one since many Khamags abandoned Jamukha soon after the battle. In 1195, the Jin Empire and the Tatars broke their longstanding alliance and fought each other in a bloody conflict, which ended with a Chinese victory. Temujin took advantage of this to attack the Tatars now that they had been much weakened, gaining a resounding victory and, quite unexpectedly, winning for himself the admiration of the Jin military commanders. During 1198 and 1199, Temujin's forces, together with the Keraites, continued attacking the Mergids and obtained a series of victories over them. In 1199, the Khamags and the Keraites invaded the territory of the Naimans, which led to the birth of a large anti-Temujin coalition that comprised both the Naimans and the Tatars. The leadership of this coalition was later assigned to Jamukha. In 1203, after several years of indecisive campaigning against his enemies, Temujin was betrayed by the Keraites, who changed side and joined forces with Jamukha. Having been abandoned by his allies, Temujin suffered various minor setbacks, but by the end of 1203 he was finally able to crush the Keraites once and for all. In 1204, Jamukha, the Mergids, the Naimans and what remained of the Keraites joined forces against Temujin. However, Temujin, now commanding over 60,000 warriors, defeated the warriors of his combined enemies at the decisive Battle of Chakirmaut.

This brilliant victory for Temujin enabled him to start the unification of all the Mongol tribal groups under his rule. In the summer of 1206, at the Onon River, the pre-eminent shaman Kokochu proclaimed Temujin 'Genghis Khan', or' 'Universal Ruler', of all the Mongol communities. This event marked the birth of a unified Mongol state, which would go on to conquer most of Asia during the following decades. Soon after becoming Universal Ruler of the Mongols, Genghis Khan started planning an invasion of the Jin Empire that dominated northern China. In 1210, he insulted the Jin Emperor by publicly stating that he was a coward and unfit to rule. The Jin monarch responded by executing the Mongol ambassador who lived at his court, thereby initiating hostilities between the Mongols and the Jin Empire. Genghis Khan assembled an impressive army of over 100,000 horsemen to invade northern China and reached the Great Wall in March 1211. Although the Jin forces garrisoning the Great Wall – which had been built some centuries before to protect China from the attacks of the nomadic peoples – outnumbered the Mongols nearly ten times, they were not capable of concentrating in the sector of the defensive line that was to be attacked by Genghis Khan. Thanks to the activities of his scouts, Genghis Khan learned that the least-defended portion of the Great Wall was the Wusha Fortress, and thus attacked in that sector. The Wusha Fortress was located near a desert ridge called Yehuling, which commanded the north-west approach to the Juyong Pass, the gateway to the Jin capital of Zhongdu (present-day Beijing). Between March and October 1211, the Mongols seized the Wusha Fortress before routing the majority of the Jin forces at the Battle of Yehuling. Following these events, the Mongol troops were reorganized and advanced on Zhongdu. The Jin capital was besieged by Genghis Khan for about four years, during which the Chinese inhabitants of the city were forced to resort to cannibalism before they finally surrendered. With the fall of Zhongdu, the Mongols could occupy a large portion of northern China. The Jin Empire, however, continued to exist south of the territories conquered by the Mongols until it too was destroyed by Genghis Khan's successors in 1234.

In 1216, following the end of his Chinese campaigns, Genghis Khan turned his attention to the conquest of Central Asia. His first targets were two nomadic states located on the borders of Mongolia, both of whose cultures were under strong Chinese influence: the Qara Khitai of the Khitans and the Western Xia of the Tanguts. The Khitans were conquered quite rapidly by the Mongols between 1216 and 1218, while the Tanguts were spared for some years and their lands were occupied by Mongol troops only during 1225–1227. At the beginning of the thirteenth century, the western portion of Central Asia's steppes was dominated by the Khwarezmid Empire, a vast Muslim state that was culturally Turko-Persian. The Khwarezmid Empire emerged in 1077, following the collapse of Turkic power in Central Asia, and in just a few decades it came to control the whole territory of present-day Iran in addition to a vast portion of the steppes located between the Caspian Sea and Mongolia. The military forces of the Khwarezmid Empire were quite numerous and strong, including sizeable numbers of Kipchak mercenaries. The Muslim state was located south of the Kipchak territories and west of the Qara Khitai. Genghis Khan considered the Khwarezmid Empire to be a strong rival power and thus mobilized large numbers of troops to occupy it. The Mongol invasion of the empire took place between 1219 and 1221 and was characterized by a series of sieges – which ended successfully for the Mongols thanks to the technical assistance provided by several Chinese experts – as well as by the terrible atrocities committed by Genghis Khan's warriors in order to intimidate their enemies. The forces of the Khwarezmid Empire were decisively defeated in 1221 at the Battle of the Indus River, following which

Mongol armoured horse archer of the Golden Horde. (*Photo by Dimitar Atanassov, IEFSEM-BAS, Experiencing History Research Project, copyright by Asociatia C.S. Nokors, Bucharest, Romania*)

Mongol armoured horse archer of the Golden Horde; note the rich incisions reproduced on the helmet. (*Photo by Dimitar Atanassov, IEFSEM-BAS, Experiencing History Research Project, copyright by Asociatia C.S. Nokors, Bucharest, Romania*)

the Mongols raided present-day Pakistan and northern India before annexing the territories of the Khwarezmid Empire to their domains. The conquest of the Central Asian state had important strategic consequences for Genghis Khan's expansionist plans, since the Mongols could now attack both the Russian princedoms in Eastern Europe and the Islamic countries in the Middle East. After the fall of their country, around 10,000 professional warriors from the Khwarezmid Army migrated to the Middle East, where they were employed as mercenaries by the various Muslim states. They served with distinction under the Seljuk Sultanate of Rum, the Arab Abbasid Caliphate, the Ayyubids of Syria and Egypt (the successors of Saladin) before being absorbed by the Mamluks after they established their own independent dynasty in Egypt.

In 1221, the Mongol troops continued their westwards advance by moving from Iran to the Caucasus, where they defeated the Alans and the Kipchaks, together with the Kingdom of Georgia. After consolidating their control over the Caucasus, the hordes of Genghis Khan attacked the Russian principalities from the south and defeated them – together with their Kipchak-Cuman allies – at the decisive Battle of the Kalka River in 1223. Quite unexpectedly, the Mongols did not attempt to occupy Russia permanently, despite having killed thousands of Russian soldiers, instead moving north by following the course of the Volga River and attacking the domains of the Volga Bulgars. In 1225, Genghis Khan regrouped his forces in Central Asia before attacking the Western Xia state. During 1227, shortly after having completed the invasion of the Western Xia territories, the great Mongol military leader – the most effective warlord in the history of the steppe peoples – died after falling from his horse during a hunt. He left behind an ever-expanding empire that was already immense, extending from the Pacific coastline of northern China in the east to the plains of southern Russia in the west. During the period 1227–1300, the warlike successors of Genghis Khan, despite dividing their territories into several autonomous Mongol states, continued their expansion across Europe and Asia. They conquered the whole of Russia, attacked Poland and Hungary several times, raided most of the Balkans, occupied the whole of Iran, annexed the Seljuk lands in the Middle East, captured Baghdad and attempted an invasion of Mameluke Egypt. They also assaulted the Dehli Sultanate in India, submitted Tibet, occupied the whole territory of China, conquered Korea, attacked Japan, assaulted Indochina and campaigned in Java. The Mongol Empire forged by Genghis Khan was the largest empire ever seen and the most long-lasting political entity created by a nomadic people. One of Genghis Khan's greatest achievements was to organize the tribal military forces of the Mongols in a proper and effective way. He transformed a mass of rugged warriors into a well-structured army, whose units were organized according to a decimal system.

The smallest Mongol military unit, the *arban*, consisted of ten men, who were commanded by an officer known as a *bagatur*. Ten *arbans* made up a larger unit known as a *jagun*, which was comparable to a squadron since it mustered 100 warriors. Ten *jaguns* made up a *minghan* of 1,000 soldiers, which was comparable to a modern regiment. Ten *minghans* could be assembled together to form the largest kind of military unit employed by the Mongols, the *tumen* of 10,000 warriors, which corresponded to a division and as such could operate as an independent army during campaigns. On most occasions, after the unification of the Mongol communities carried out by Genghis Khan, a Mongol army consisted of two or three *tumens* (20,000–30,000 men). Transfer from one unit to another was strictly forbidden, and each warrior was tasked with performing a specific function. Each able-bodied Mongol man was a warrior and as such he was liable for military service between the ages of 14 and 60. While in the field, each Mongol army was divided into three main forces: the left wing (or *Junghar*), the right wing (or *Baraunghar*) and the centre (or

Mongol armoured horse archer of the Golden Horde firing his composite bow. (*Photo by Dimitar Atanassov, IEFSEM-BAS, Experiencing History Research Project, copyright by Asociatia C.S. Nokors, Bucharest, Romania*)

Detail of composite bow used by a Mongol archer of the Golden Horde. (*Photo by Dimitar Atanassov, IEFSEM-BAS, Experiencing History Research Project, copyright by Asociatia C.S. Nokors, Bucharest, Romania*)

Khol). Within the Mongol military there was also an elite Imperial Guard called the *Keshik*, for the formation of which the finest troops were selected. Initially, Genghis Khan's guard was made up of his personal followers, who came from his same clan or tribal group, but over time the Imperial Guard was greatly enlarged and came to comprise around 10,000 elite warriors. By the end of Genghis Khan's reign, all the sons of the officers commanding *jaguns* and *minghans* were automatically accepted into the ranks of the *Keshik*, with the other places available in the elite corps being allocated on a competitive basis and thus assigned to the common Mongol warriors who distinguished themselves in battle. The Imperial Guard acted as a military academy for the Mongol army, since – in addition to acting as an elite force that was placed under the direct orders of the *khan* – it also worked as a training school for its members. A fully trained guardsman was reckoned fit to command a *tumen* and had precedence over the commander of a *minghan*. The members of the Imperial Guard enjoyed a series of special privileges compared with the other Mongol warriors, but they were obliged to serve also in peacetime since they formed a permanent military contingent with a professional nature. When it became an elite *tumen* with 10,000 warriors, the Imperial Guard started to comprise a *minghan*, which was tasked with performing as the inner bodyguard of Genghis Khan. All the units of the Mongol army, from the smallest to the largest, were drawn from a mixture of clans and tribes in order to ensure that their members' loyalty would be to the *khan* and not to a specific component of the Mongolian communities.

When Genghis Khan was present at the head of his troops, they marched under a special standard known as a *tuk*, a special yak-tail standard that could be used only by the *khan*. The *khan* usually had complete trust in his military commanders and gave them great autonomy while operating in the field. The general strategy was decided by the *khan*, but the tactics required to put it into action could be chosen without external interference by the various field commanders. These commanders transmitted their orders to the various units placed under their command by means of a great drum (the *naccara*), which also acted as a symbol of their rank. Mongol society was quite egalitarian, even before the ascendancy of Genghis Khan. Although there were some leading families having aristocratic status – which guided the various clans and tribes – skill at warfare counted far more highly than aristocratic birth. Genghis Khan augmented the degree of meritocracy that was present in the Mongol military forces, for example by promoting to the rank of officer all the common warriors who distinguished themselves in battle. Strict discipline was a key factor behind the many victories of the Mongols, and this was enforced through some very harsh methods via a military code that prescribed a series of different corporal punishments. Frequent inspections were carried out to monitor the condition of each warrior's personal equipment. Contrary to popular belief, the Mongol armies that conquered most of Asia and Eastern Europe were not always numerically superior to their opponents. Indeed, it was very difficult for the Mongol commanders invading a distant country to obtain sufficient reinforcements from their motherland. The standard Mongol method of reinforcing armies in the field was to absorb defeated enemies, especially if these came from nomadic peoples who were culturally similar to the Mongols. The Mongol armies consisted entirely of cavalry, which comprised large numbers of horse archers supported by smaller contingents of heavy cavalrymen.

The great mobility of the Mongol military contingents was more than a match for their enemies, being part of the Mongols' traditional lifestyle. All the Mongol communities lived in tents known as *yurts*, which were made of black felt mounted on a collapsible wicker framework. The *yurts* were extremely light and easy to carry,

Detail of sabre used by a Mongol archer of the Golden Horde. (*Photo by Dimitar Atanassov, IEFSEM-BAS, Experiencing History Research Project, copyright by Asociatia C.S. Nokors, Bucharest, Romania*)

Mongol *keshig* (bodyguard) of the Golden Horde wearing wide-brimmed cap made of leather. (*Photo by Dean Nedialkov, Bulgaria, copyright by Asociatia C.S. Nokors, Bucharest, Romania*)

being perfectly suited to the nomadic life of the Mongols. They were carried from place to place in one piece on heavy carts, which transported all the goods of a Mongol family. The economy of the Mongols was not based on agriculture but on all kinds of domesticated animals: the Mongols herded sheep and goats for milk, meat, wool and skins, as well as cattle for milk, meat and hides. They also herded great numbers of riding horses, which played a fundamental role in controlling such large herds over the vast distances of the steppes. The Mongols, being nomadic herdsmen, moved with their extended families across the vast plains of their territories in order to seek the best opportunities for grazing and trading as the seasons changed. The extended families were grouped into clans, whose numerical consistency usually fluctuated greatly since families could move from one group to another according to circumstances. Quite often, the number of families making up a clan increased during summer and decreased during winter, depending on the availability of pasture. Each clan or group worked as a herding camp and had its own hereditary pastures. Driving their grazing herds before them, the Mongols trundled onwards with their families and all their goods by following set migratory routes and using traditional camping grounds. A young Mongol learned how to endure cold, hunger and thirst from his early years. The Mongol lifestyle was also characterized by continuous skirmishes with the other nomadic communities that took place in the steppes. Plundering expeditions were extremely common, robbing animals from the camps of rival groups. Large cavalry battles could be fought for the capture of camping grounds, as controlling one of these could determine the survival of an entire clan. Mongol boys were taught from an early age to ride horses both with and without saddles, as well as to use the deadly composite bow of the steppes with great precision. The Mongols were excellent hunters – being masters at doing so with hawks and eagles – and thus their composite bows were also used for hunting purposes. By grouping their herds and by hunting in the steppe plains, they practiced the same movements and actions on which their battle tactics were based. The composite bow represented the greatest empowerment for a Mongol individual over the environment in which he lived. A young Mongol, for example, had to master the use of the horse and the composite bow in order to persuade the elders of his clan that he might – in time – become an effective horse archer.

The Mongols prepared their campaigns with great care and attention, for example by examining all the possible weak points of their opponents' forces through an effective network of scouts and spies. These scouts also collected vital information concerning roads, weather conditions and possible grazing grounds that was of fundamental importance for the invasion of a foreign country. The Mongols became infamous for their massacres of civilians, which were perpetrated across Eastern

Europe and Asia. However, these acts were not committed without reason, being part of the psychological warfare conducted by the Mongols. They terrorized their enemies by showing a level of cruelty that was otherwise unknown in the sedentary civilizations of the Middle Ages. Differently from the other nomadic peoples, the Mongols could also campaign during the winter months, as they were used to extremely cold temperatures. Their main sources of supplies while on campaign were the countries they planned to invade, but livestock was often driven on the hoof, while significant amounts of reserve weapons were also transported by camels of the steppes or by pack-horses. The horse breeds living in the steppes of the Mongols could be fed on virtually any quality of pasturage, since they were capable of fending for themselves in the very severe conditions of their natural environment. Coping well and gaining sustenance for their horses gave a decisive advantage to mounted warriors during extended campaigns like those conducted by the Mongols, as their mounts did not require the carting of fodder but were simply let loose at the end of a day's riding to fend for themselves. The ugly appearance of the Mongol horses was compensated by their resilience, which impressed contemporary Christian and Muslim observers. The small and sturdy ponies of the Mongols were far better at climbing, jumping and swimming than the horses of their opponents; they were used to living in a semi-wild way and thus could endure any hardship. The Mongols, like several other nomadic peoples, made a practice of travelling with a number of reserve horses to ensure that they always had a fresh mount when needed. They were capable of riding with no interruptions for an entire day, meaning they could travel enormous distances in a relatively short period of time, eating only some cured meat that was transported under their saddles.

When invading a foreign territory, the Mongols usually advanced in widely separated columns before concentrating their forces into a single point when a decisive battle had to be fought. In every Mongol military camp there were always at least two horses kept saddled for the sending of messages, while smoke signals could also be used to communicate messages. Each Mongol army had large numbers of scouts operating up to 70 miles ahead of its main body, as well as on the its flanks and to the rear. The screens of explorers provided a constant supply of information to the commanders and operated in a wholly autonomous way. The standard battle formation of the Mongols consisted of five ranks: the two front ones were made up of armoured heavy cavalrymen, while the remaining three ranks comprised horse archers. When a battle began, the mounted archers advanced through the gaps in the heavy cavalry formations and poured a devastating volley of arrows into the enemy ranks. At the same time, either or both the wings of the horse archers began an encircling movement aimed at taking their enemies in the flank or in the rear. This movement was known as the *tulughma*, or 'standard sweep'. If the attack of the light cavalrymen was repulsed, they calmly withdrew but continued to shoot arrows as they went (since Mongol horse archers were trained to perform the famous 'Parthian shot', turning and firing arrows backwards while riding). Usually, after a few repeated attacks of the horse archers, the formations of the Mongols' enemies fell into disorder. It was at this point that the Mongol heavy cavalry would launch a frontal charge, which usually decided the outcome of the battle. All these battle movements were carried out with perfect order and in complete silence, with orders being communicated by the raising and lowering of black and white flags or by using lanterns when a battle took place at night. When present on the battlefield, the Imperial Guard – the members of which were heavily armoured – was usually kept in reserve and was employed only to deal with any enemy counter-attacks. No army knew better than the Mongols how important it was to pursue a defeated enemy, and thus they usually harassed their fleeing opponents for days over many miles. Mongol armies were also well known for the use they made of the nomadic tactic known as the feigned retreat, which was accompanied by a series of other tricks such as stirring up dust clouds to simulate the presence of additional troops. The Mongols believed themselves to be invincible, but during their early campaigns fought outside the steppes they

Mongol horse archer. (*Colour plate by Patricio Greve Moller, copyright by Gabriele Esposito*)

Mongol horse archer of the Golden Horde. (*Photo by Dean Nedialkov, Bulgaria, copyright by Asociatia C.S. Nokors, Bucharest, Romania*)

experienced serious problems while besieging enemy fortifications because they had very little experience of siege warfare. With the progression of time, however, they learned from experience and started to build impressive siege machines under the supervision of Chinese or Muslim military advisors.

The physical appearance of the Mongol warriors shocked many contemporary Christian and Muslim observers during the early thirteenth century, since it was not common for the inhabitants of Europe or the Middle East to see 'wild' people from the steppes of the Far East and who practiced a pagan religion that was unknown outside Mongolia. The Mongols had broad faces, flat noses, prominent cheekbones, slit eyes, thick lips, thin beards, straight black hair and swarthy skin tanned by sun and wind. They were also short of stature, and their stocky, heavy bodies were supported by bow legs. The Mongols usually shaved a square on top of their heads, and from the front corners of this square they shaved seams down to their temples, which were also shaved, as was the neck up to the point where it joins the skull (thus leaving a broken ring of hair around the head). The lock of hair left on the forehead was allowed to grow and hung down as far as the eyebrows. The hair remaining on the scalp was wound into two plaits, which were knotted behind each ear. The basic 'national' costume of the Mongols was very practical, being designed to protect the body from extremely cold temperatures, for example in the choice of furs and padded clothing. The standard Mongol headgear was a cap with a conical shape and made of quilted material or cloth. It had a large turned-up brim that could be folded down in times of cold weather; sometimes the brim was divided in two parts. The Mongol cap was often lined with fox, wolf or lynx skin, or could be lined with plush fabric. Earflaps were quite common too. The main garment worn by a Mongol warrior was his long robe-like coat, which opened from top to bottom, with; the left breast doubling over the right side, where it was fastened by a button or a tie located a few inches below the right armpit. The Mongol coats had wide sleeves, which were long in the winter coats made from sheepskin and short in the summer ones made of cotton. A shirt-like undergarment, which was very simple and comfortable, was usually worn under the coat. For the richest warriors who acted as officers, this shirt could be made of silk and have rich decorative embroidering. Mongol trousers were wide and tucked into stout leather boots, which did not have heels but thick soles made of felt. The boots were fastened by long laces. During the winter, Mongol warriors wore thick felt socks and one or two fur coats over the standard coat described above. One of the fur coats was worn with the fur in contact with the skin and the other with the fur on the outside (exposed to wind and snow). The Mongols generally obtained furs from the skins of bears, wolves and foxes, but the poorest individuals could get them from the skins of dogs and goats. During winter, the usual trousers were replaced by special

Mongol horse archer. (*Colour plate by Patricio Greve Moller, copyright by Gabriele Esposito*)

ones made of felt, and the richest warriors insulated their clothing with silk stuffing (which was very light but warm). The common warriors, meanwhile, lined their clothes with cotton cloth or with the fine wool that they picked out of the coarser wool used for making felt. Each Mongol warrior carried two leather bottles, which were filled with dried horse milk curd mixed with water, which produced a sort of watery yogurt that was greatly appreciated by the Mongols. While on campaign, each Mongol warrior usually carried a light axe that was used as a working tool, a file for sharpening the arrowheads that was fastened to the quiver, a horsehair lasso that could be employed as a cavalry weapon, a coil of stout rope, an awl, a needle and thread, a cooking pot made of iron or earthenware and the two leather bottles already described above. Mongol warriors also had a large bag made of soft leather that was closed by a long thong; this was used to keep clothes and other equipment dry while crossing rivers, being tied to the horse's tail. Each basic military unit of ten men slept in the same tent made of felt. The sturdy Mongol horses, having dense coats that kept them warm during winter, had a simple but effective equipment that comprised a firm saddle, which weighed about 10lb and was high at the back and front. The saddle was rubbed with sheep's fat to prevent swelling in the rain. The

Mongol horse archer of the Golden Horde.
(*Photo by Dean Nedialkov, Bulgaria, copyright by Asociatia C.S. Nokors, Bucharest, Romania*)

Mongol stirrups were extremely solid and slung from very short straps.

The main weapon of the Mongol horse archers was the composite bow, which had a pull of 166lb and a destructive range of 200–300 yards. Each Mongol warrior usually carried a longer bow and a shorter one, plus two or three quivers holding about thirty arrows each. The arrows could be of two different kinds: light arrows with small and sharp points that were designed for long-range shooting or heavy arrows with large and broad points that were designed for shooting over short ranges. The arrowheads were hardened by heating them until they became red-hot and then dipping them into salt water, a treatment that made them hard enough to pierce armour. The shafts of the arrows were usually fletched with eagle feathers. Instead of the composite bow, the heavy cavalrymen were armed with a long spear fitted with a hook for pulling enemies from the saddle (a weapon that the Mongols probably copied from the Chinese). Mongol heavy spears were designed for thrusting and were extremely powerful. They were used with just one hand, since most of the Mongol heavy cavalrymen also carried a small round shield that was made of skin or wicker and offered good protection against enemy arrows. The Mongol heavy cavalrymen also carried various offensive weapons designed for hand-

Mongol infantryman. (*Colour plate by Patricio Greve Moller, copyright by Gabriele Esposito*)

to-hand fighting, which included maces and short axes. All Mongol warriors, be they horse archers or heavy cavalrymen, were equipped with a light sabre that was very similar to that used by the Cumans and Kipchaks, the Mongols having copied it from the Turkic peoples of the steppes. The Mongol heavy cavalrymen protected themselves with various types of cuirass; they could be made from leather or iron *lamellae*. Following the Mongol expansion into Eastern Europe and the Middle East, however, chainmail also started to be used by them. Leather armour was made by joining various sections together in order to make a tough and flexible plate, the leather having first been softened by boiling. Leather armour was weatherproofed by covering it with a crude lacquer made from pitch. It was often worn only on the front of the body, consisting of a simple corselet. This kind of armour was usually employed by the poorest warriors of the heavy cavalry. Lamellar armour was made by taking a number of thin iron plates – a finger's breadth wide and a hand's breadth long – and piercing eight holes in each plate. A series of such plates were then bound together by leather thongs in order to create numerous strips that were later joined to make an armour plate. The lamellar armour of the Mongols was extremely difficult to pierce but very flexible, thanks to its peculiar construction. It was polished so brightly that it was said one could see one's reflection in it. The lamellar armour plates were made up into suits, which included a long coat reaching well below the knees. This opened all down the front and was fastened as far down as the waist (no doubt for convenience in riding). A lamellar armour plate was worn on each shoulder and was fastened to the coat, thus completing the suit. Several of the richest warriors, especially the officers who usually equipped themselves as heavy cavalry, wore decorative surcoats over their armour. These were produced in bright colours and could have complex decorations. The helmets of the Mongol heavy cavalry had a segmented construction and a central spike or round ball on the top, which was surmounted by coloured feathers or horsehair and often bent towards the rear. Most of the Mongol helmets had very wide neck-guards made of iron *lamellae* applied on a leather aventail, which were designed for protection against enemy arrows. Sometimes they were large enough to reach around under the chin. Over time, both cheek-pieces and nasals were added to the helmets of the Mongol heavy cavalry, which already had a special plate placed on the front that comprised a brim and protected the eyebrows. In most cases, the horses of the Mongol heavy cavalry were armoured, being protected by lamellar cuirasses. These consisted of five sections: one on either side of the horse, which stretched from the tail to the base of the neck and were fastened to the saddle; the third one behind the saddle on the back of the horse; the fourth on the horse's neck; and the fifth on the breast. The forehead of the horse was protected by an iron plate consisting of a single piece of metal.

Bibliography

Anderson, E.B., *Cataphracts: Knights of the Ancient Eastern Empires* (Pen & Sword, 2016).

Brzezinski, R. and Mielczarek, M., *The Sarmatians 600 BC–AD 450* (Osprey Publishing, 2002).

Cernenko, E.V., *The Scythians 700–300 BC* (Osprey Publishing, 1983).

Fields, N., *The Hun* (Osprey Publishing, 2006).

Gorelik, K., *Warriors of Eurasia* (Montvert Publishing, 1995).

Heath, I., *Armies of Feudal Europe 1066–1300* (Wargames Research Group, 1989).

Heath, I., *Armies of the Dark Ages 600–1066* (Wargames Research Group, 1980).

Karasulas, A., *Mounted Archers of the Steppe 600 BC–AD 1300* (Osprey Publishing, 2004).

Nicolle, D., *Armies of Medieval Russia 750–1250* (Osprey Publishing, 1999).

Nicolle, D., *Attila and the Nomad Horses* (Osprey Publishing, 1990).

Nicolle, D., *Hungary and the Fall of Eastern Europe 1000–1568* (Osprey Publishing, 1988).

Nicolle, D. and Shpakovski, V., *Armies of the Volga Bulgars and Khanate of Kazan* (Osprey Publishing, 2013).

Nicolle, D. and Zhirohov, M., *The Khazars* (Osprey Publishing, 2019).

Nikonorov, V.P., *The Armies of Bactria 700 BC–AD 450* (Montvert Publications, 1997).

Turnbull, S., *Mongol Warrior 1200–1350* (Osprey Publishing, 2003).

Turnbull, S., *The Mongols* (Osprey Publishing, 1980).

The Re-enactors who Contributed to this Book

Iloncsuk Szabadcsapat

The meaning of the word '*Iloncsuk*' can be traced back to Turkish origins, meaning 'snake'. The Iloncsuk clan ruled the plains around Kecskemét (Hungary), and this is where our name comes from. The association was founded in 1998 in Kunszentmiklós. In the beginning, we worked as an archery team and then the attention of the members turned to close combat. Since our establishment, we have been trying to present the glory of the Kuns to the interested public. The main profile of our team is to present the costumes, weaponry and lifestyle of the Kuns who settled in the area with Khan Kötöny, and the turbulent decades and centuries that followed. The closest to the modern era is the Jászkun National Guard, which takes you back to the 1848/49 War of Independence. We try to present the different periods as authentically as possible. The members of the team are also involved in various handicraft activities (leatherwork, forging, horseshoeing and knife-making). We have organized our last year on the basis of less is sometimes more. By this we mean that we cannot meet every request, but where we can we try to participate with all our might. Over the years, we have participated in many small and large traditional commemorations and events. Fortunately, we have also had several requests for documentaries, such as *Regnum Fest* and *Alone against the Great Mongol Empire*. Our association is looking to the future with unbroken enthusiasm and confidence for such and similar requests.

Contacts:
Email: Iloncsuk01@outlook.hu
Facebook: https://www.facebook.com/Iloncsukszabadcsapat/

Isenbrand Saga

The 'Isenbrand Saga' is a living history-based project, focusing on the central decades of the fifth century AD, i.e. the last years of the reign of Attila the Hun. The project has three main elements: the first is fifth century living history activity, the second is a novel (planned to be part of a series) about Isenbrand – the Warrior of Attila – and movies produced under the name of the Isenbrand Saga. I'm a 35-year-old information technologist in love with storytelling and history. I started to research and to work on my Germanic gear after I got the chance to impersonate Attila the Hun in a documentary. I think storytelling is the most effective way to spread historical facts and we are in a great need to do so. We have much incorrect information about the Huns and we usually forget that the Hunnic Empire consisted of different peoples having different origins. The Hunnic Empire became great only because it allowed different cultures to merge into a strong unity. Through the Isenbrand Saga project I wanted to tell a story about heroism, loyalty and honour seasoned with some other elements: a bit of supernatural, intrigue and betrayal. Isenbrand, a warrior of Attila the Hun, becomes a toy of fate: his captain betrays him, then he loses everything step by step. Meanwhile, he gets into trouble with a mysterious killer, monsters lurking in the night and the scheming of some nobles. And above his head hovers the sword of doom: he learns that Attila's life is in danger, and if the great king dies, the empire will perish with him.

Contacts:
Website: https://www.patreon.com/Isenbrandsaga
Facebook: https://www.facebook.com/isenbrandsaga

Nyugati Gyepűk Pajzsa Haditorna Egyesület

The 'Nyugati Gyepűk Pajzsa' group researches and exercises the combat of the elite armoured cavalry units of the tenth century from the Grand Duchy of Hungary. It places great emphasis on the authentic recreation and application of equestrian armour and close combat weapons, as well as on the authentic equestrian equipment and riding techniques. The team is special because it uses scientifically sophisticated equipment and weapon reconstructions to fight in realistic close combat on horseback, free-fight style, and strives to make the fighting techniques as authentic as possible to be near the originals.

Contacts:
Website: https://nyugatigyepu.hu/
Email: nyugatigyepukpajzsa@gmail.com
Facebook: https://www.facebook.com/people/Nyugati-Gyep%C5%B1k-Pajzsa-Haditorna-Egyes%C3%BClet/100064818606119/

Hungarian-Turán Foundation

The Hungarian-Turán Foundation is the largest traditionalist organization in Hungary. It consists of two parts: a traditionalist one with military traditionalists, folk musicians, craftsmen, equestrian traditionalists and horse breeders; and a scientific one with scientific researchers in history, archaeology, anthropology, genetics, ethnography and linguistics. The researchers of the Foundation all respect Hungarian traditions and culture, but at the same time their research proceeds exclusively along the lines of modern science. With the symbolic term 'Turán', the Foundation conveys that it is not only researching the history of Hungarians in the Carpathian Basin, but also the migration of Hungarians outside the Basin, the early stages of their ethnogenesis (leading to distant, even Asian regions) and their kinship relations. The Hungarian-Turán Foundation has extensive connections with professionals and traditionalists in various countries (Romania, Ukraine and the Republic of Moldova), but especially in related countries such as: Turkey, Kazakhstan, Azerbaijan, Uzbekistan, Turkmenistan, Kyrgyzstan, Mongolia and the member republics of the Russian Federation: Bashkiria, Tatarstan, Dagestan, Kabardino-Balkaria, Karachay-Cherkessia, Buryatia, Altai Republic, Tuva and Yakutia. The Foundation considers its task to present scientific results to a non-expert audience, as well as to help Hungarian traditionalist groups establish contact with similar organizations of related peoples. It also supports the high-quality organization and implementation of joint programmes. The Hungarian-Turán Foundation organizes many traditional sports (ethnosports) programmes (archery, falconry, horse riding skills, wrestling, etc.) and similar activities. The events organized by the Foundation – the Kurultaj Hungarian Tribal Gathering and the Day of the Ancestors – are the largest tradition-preserving events in Europe since 2012.

Contacts:
Email: info@hungarian-turan.hu
Website: https://kurultaj.hu/
Facebook: https://www.facebook.com/kurultaj

Association for Restoration and Preservation of Bulgarian Traditions – Avitohol

We are a non-profit association for public benefit, established in 2012 with headquarters in the city of Varna, Bulgaria. The main goal of the association is the study of the historical heritage, martial culture, way of life and culture of the Bulgarians during the Middle Ages. The association organizes and conducts events – festivals, assemblies, seminars and forums – contributing to the development and promotion of the historical and cultural-living heritage, uniting the efforts of a large part of the re-enactors in Bulgaria, together with archaeologists, historians and scientists. An important task of the Association is to develop research and reconstruction activities on Bulgarians during the early Middle Ages, the seventh to tenth centuries, to study their places of residence, way of life and culture, military and equestrian traditions and combat practices. The members of the association build historical reconstructions of clothing, weapons and equipment, working hard to achieve maximum authenticity of the reconstruction, working with a wide range of masters of ancient crafts – blacksmiths, tanners, weavers, potters, etc. – to restore combat practices on foot and from horseback, thanks to the opportunity to work with horses, striving to present their reconstruction fully and thoroughly to the public. Over the last 12 years, the association has organized more than 170 events, including more than 100 festivals and assemblies on historical topics, including the periods of Antiquity, Early and Late Middle Ages, and more than seventy events including exhibitions of historical reconstructions, seminars and open lessons for students, archery tournaments, etc., while participating in other events in the country and abroad. We have also been to over fifty festivals and tournaments over the years.

Contacts:
Website: www.avitohol.org
Email: jasminparvanov@gmail.com
Facebook: https://www.facebook.com/avitohol12/

Equestrian Martial Arts School – Madara Horseman

The Madara Horseman project started as an idea to create a modern sport (martial art) based on historical tradition, combining horse, dog and human handling of the main ancient weapons. In the process, several main directions of development took shape, training horses, training people in the specific riding that we call 'combat', training in working with different types of weapons and training a dog. A strong point in the school's work is the master's methods, which have been developed over the years for training people in combat riding, archery, spear and sabre work. Another strong direction in the school's work is the socialization, training and preparation of children and the specifics of the school's activities. The successful work of the school in creating modern methods based on historical traditions in the field of martial arts on horseback and on foot has been appreciated over the years with numerous invitations to hold seminars and trainings in a number of countries worldwide. Dimitar Trukanov, who is the founder of the school, was awarded the highest instructor degree in horseback archery by the International Federation of Equestrian Archery, with only three mounted archers in the world having this degree.

Contacts:
Email: trukan@abv.bg
Facebook: https://www.facebook.com/profile.php?id=100066814110050
https://www.facebook.com/dimitar.trukanov

Bulgarian School of Ancient Military Arts – Greatness

The Bulgarian School of Ancient Military Arts – Greatness is an association for historical re-enactment of two major periods of Bulgarian history: Antiquity and the Middle Ages. The main goal of the School is the recreation of the ancient martial culture of the Bulgarians and its values, through the exercise of the body in historical forms of armed struggle. This is an educational and creative activity, a means of personal experience of the ancient cultural forms of Antiquity and the Middle Ages and their preservation in the form of Ancient War Games – Areti. A highlight of the School's activity is the creation of the School of Old Bulgarian Sabre, which aims to revive and preserve historical sabre fighting from the Bulgarian Middle Ages and make it part of the world of today's popular Historical Fencing and Historical European Martial Arts (HEMA). The ancient martial arts practiced at the school are presented to the general public in the form of combat demonstration, battle re-enactment and historical martial sports. Fighters from the school take part in chains of tournaments, according to the rules of the HMBIA (International Association for Historical Medieval Combat), IFAA (International Archery Association/FA) and IAF (International Falconry Organization) etc. The Bulgarian School of Ancient Military Arts – Greatness also conducts cultural and educational activities. Among them are: Sky Fighters falcon competitions, New Beginning and Odryuza – the Cradle of a Thousand Cities – historical gatherings, traditional archery tournament Historical Park and many others.

Contacts:
Email: m.petrov@ipark.bg
Facebook: https://www.facebook.com/school.velichie

Jordan Sivkov – Leather Works

Jordan Sivkov has been engaged in re-enactment since 2008. Initially, his interest was focused on researching and making the clothes of the Bulgarians and other peoples from the early Middle Ages, the seventh to tenth centuries. In 2010, he participated for the first time in a historical festival in Asenovgrad, Bulgaria, and then in 2012 in the festival in Pliska, Bulgaria. These participations started his research activity, which led to the creation of a site dedicated to the clothing of the Bulgarians from the early Middle Ages, which was met with great interest by the re-enactor community in Bulgaria and served as a benchmark for increasing the authenticity of historical re-enactment. Interest in the site provoked Jordan to collect more data and after three years of research activity, conversations with many archaeologists and historians, attempts to understand how the people of that time thought and answering the question 'why so?', he created a new, detailed and expanded site version. In the process of collecting data, he researches literature related to Antiquity and the Middle Ages, which is where his interest in nomadic peoples such as the Scythians, Huns, Avars, Bulgarians, Pechenegs and Cumans comes from. He focuses his re-enactor activity on the Huns and Scythians because of their interesting way of life. With the reconstruction of Huns and Scythians, he has participated in festivals in Bulgaria and abroad. He has taken part in medieval festivals as a Bulgarian warrior or as a Cuman. Since 2015, he has been making leather items for the purposes of historical reconstruction – leather accessories, bags, belts, shoes and boots – which he says he enjoys doing. His reconstructions of leather accessories, shoes and boots are renowned in re-enactor circles worldwide.

Contacts:
Email: sivkov.jordan@gmail.com
Facebook: https://www.facebook.com/jordan.sivkov/
https://www.facebook.com/Jordan.Sivkov.Leatherworks/

Kalina Atanasova

Kalina Atanasova has a PhD degree in Bulgarian medieval archaeology. She is the author of a monograph and several scientific articles. Their subject matter comprises the clothing during the First and Second Bulgarian Empires and the Byzantine period, which includes the settling of the so-called late nomads on the Balkans. Under the alias Badamba, the author and her team have been making reconstructions and replicas of historical costumes for re-enactors, museum expositions and thematic exhibitions since 2006. Some of them can be viewed on her website. In the form of a travelling exhibition, living pictures (scenes from history) and lectures, the results of their work also participate in historical festivals in Bulgaria, Romania and Serbia, helping to present to the public visually and interactively the way of life and culture of the Bulgarians from the twelfth to fourteenth century.

Contacts:
Website: https://badamba.info/workshop/en_index.html
Email: kalina@badamba.info

Boris Bedrosov

Boris Bedrosov has been a part of the Bulgarian re-enactment scene for about two decades. Although his main field of interest is the military life of the Second Bulgarian Empire and early stages of Ottoman rule (late twelfth to mid-fifteenth century), he is also fascinated by the military history of the Balkans for a very long period – from the ninth century to the Second World War. Since a very young age, he has loved to make things by his own hands. Starting as a hobby in 2006, when he made his first helmet and shield, there has been a significant evolution in his skills and craftsmanship. Now he is able to create beautiful, accurate and detailed historical reproductions of a wide variety of knives, daggers, swords and other medieval weapons, helmets, armour and shields. They are never made 'in series', but are hand-made and unique. He is continually learning new armouring techniques, because he believes in continual personal development and growth. He always searches for new challenges and loves making new pieces. The main rules in his work are: 1) hand-work – every element of his products is made using only high quality materials (although he uses power tools, he constantly tries to make by hand as many details as possible); 2) historical accuracy – he makes his pieces based purely on historical finds, extant original pieces or depictions from period sources; 3) attention to detail – his pieces are as close as possible in appearance to the originals in construction, shape, detail and decoration, or meet the specific customer's demand.

Contacts:
Email: bbedrosov@abv.bg
Facebook: https://www.facebook.com/borisbedrosovarmoury

Asociatia C.S. Nokors

Nokors (from '*nökör*', the Mongolian word for 'companion' or 'friend') is a historical re-enactment (living history) group. It was established in 2018 as a public association, registered as a legal entity. There are two major directions in historical research and re-enactment that Nokors follows: material culture of the Golden Horde – a nomadic community of the thirteenth to fourteenth century – and material culture of the citizens of the Golden Horde (officials, merchants and artisans), including the population of the 'national' non-Mongol communities – Venetians, Genoese, Wallachians, Moldavians and Bulgars. Minor directions of our research include reconstructing the material culture of the nomadic peoples living during the first to ninth century AD. To be able to recreate the daily life of a nomadic society, we try to reproduce as accurately as possible the dressing habits and weaponry, everyday carrying (EDC) and common items used on a daily basis, such as living quarters, hairdressing and food habits. Nokors is interested in spreading cultural and historical information for the benefit of the public viewer, by presenting a realistic depiction of the nomadic life that can reach as many people as possible. We attend historical festivals and cultural events, where we carry out workshops open to the public for painting, calligraphy, sewing techniques, archery and medicinal plants. We are on a continuous path of improving our knowledge, so we strive to be updated on the most recent historical and archaeological finds. Nokors is mostly interested in research of the Tatar influence in the Dobrogea area and the various ways Tatar culture influenced Romanian history.

Contacts:
E-mail: nokors1330@gmail.com
Facebook: https://www.facebook.com/nokors1330

Hrafn Vaeringi

Hrafn Vaeringi is a renowned combat sports group based in the United Kingdom, specializing in the portrayal of warriors from the tenth and eleventh centuries. With impressive experience in engagements throughout the UK and Europe, the group prides itself on fostering a strong sense of camaraderie and familial bonds among its members. Encouraging individuals to craft their own narratives through the mastery of sword, axe or spear combat, Hrafn Vaeringi has cultivated a community built on the foundation of martial artistry. Through the art of combat, the group has not only forged enduring connections but also a profound collective identity, akin to that of a tight-knit family. The valour and prowess demonstrated by members both on and off the battlefield have garnered widespread recognition, with the tales of their triumphs resonating far beyond geographical boundaries. Hrafn Vaeringi's fighters are celebrated globally for their remarkable achievements, solidifying the group's esteemed reputation in the realm of combat sports. As a collective of dedicated and skilled warriors, Hrafn Vaeringi exemplifies the fusion of historical authenticity with a contemporary spirit, embodying the timeless ideals of honour, discipline and kinship. Their unwavering commitment to their craft and their ability to weave captivating narratives through the art of combat serve as testaments to the indelible impact of their endeavours.

Contacts:
Facebook: https://www.facebook.com/hrafnvaeringi

The Skjaldborg

Founded during 1994 in Omaha (Nebraska), the Skjaldborg is a Viking Age living history group. Comprised of exclusive members as well as of individuals who hold membership in other groups and hobbies, we allow access to our group to all those enthusiasts who share in a love and a passion for the Viking Age, whether it is recreating the arts and crafts of the period or fighting for the crowd with our signature Live, Steel Combat. With our group motto of 'Many Shields, One Family', we have created a tight-knit group that strives to help each member improve in kit or combat, as well as strengthening ties in the 'real' world outside of the hobby. Another signature feature we are proud to hold is the ability to join and work together on our group mission without a jarl, king, or other sort of group hierarchy. We are all free men and women coming together without oaths or owed dues. While the group was founded in Omaha, we have since grown to encompass most of The Heartland in the United States, with members and units in Iowa, Missouri, Wisconsin, Minnesota, Illinois, Ohio and beyond. We are always open to new members seeking to join with us. As with most groups, we also started with a few tents in a field at events. Due to our generous benefactors and friends, we were allowed to build our very own Viking trade home in the Danish capital of the US in Elk Horn, Iowa. We also help run, maintain and build at the Ravensborg Viking Longfort, the very first longfort in America. As the years pass by, the Skjaldborg will continue to strive for better combat demonstrations, crafting displays and contributions to our community and public. We hope you enjoy the pictures provided to this great work and hope to hear from anyone who wants to reach out to us. We want to give special thanks to every one of our photographers who provided their skills and expertise to this project: Megan Yenter of Darling Muse Photos, Matt DiGirolamo of The Ancient Armory, Kolla Mánadóttir, Daina Faulhaber, Cat Adams, Christian Pearson, Philip Ryan and Amy Studer of the Skjaldborg.

Contacts:
E-mail: skjaldborgvikings@gmail.com
Facebook: https://www.facebook.com/theskjaldborg/

Amages Drachen

Amages Drachen is a re-enactment group created by means of the living history, i.e. through reconstructions of clothing and artefacts, to make living history tangible. Our members come from the Rhine-Main area and the Stuttgart area and are committed to teaching and depicting ancient steppe cultures. Both Scythian and Sarmatian representations from a period of about 600 BC up to approximately AD 300, which we have produced on the basis of archaeological finds and historical sources, are part of our repertoire. We would like to introduce event visitors to the material culture of ancient steppe nomads with self-created replicas, explanations and lectures. The steppe belt today includes, amongst others, large parts of Ukraine, Russia, Kazakhstan, Kyrgyzstan and Mongolia, and was inhabited in ancient times by nomadic tribes; in particular, the Scythians, Saka, Sauromatians and Sarmatians, who are also part of our representations. Unfortunately, these nomadic cultures have left no written records of themselves. The knowledge of these scripture-free cultures can today only be taken from archaeological finds and written sources of neighbouring cultures. From the first millennium BC until late Antiquity, these ancient nomads stood in constant contact with the settled 'high cultures' on the edge of the steppe belt: Persians, Chinese, Greeks and Romans. These cultural contacts were both peaceful and warlike: on the one hand, the nomads benefited from the trade routes through the steppe areas (Silk Road); on the other hand, the mounted archers were also dreaded warriors or coveted mercenaries. Despite this, these 'mer-milkers' and 'horse-bowers', as they were called by ancient authors, are still rarely found in the current knowledge of history, but they have always had a decisive influence on European history and have contributed to shape the present-day face of Europe.

Contacts:
E-mail: amages.drachen@gmx.de
Website: https://www.sarmaten-steppenkultur.de/index.php/en/home-3/

Les Seigneurs d'Orient

The Lords of the Orient (Les Seigneurs d'Orient) is an historical re-enacting club based in Menton, France, since 2017. Our thirty-strong membership has many history students and teachers. Our area of expertise is the twelfth-century Near East, especially the Oriental Latin States (Outre Mer/Holy Land). We re-enact both Jerusalem's royal court and a Syrian Emir's court, with a camp, furniture, civil and military outfits and workshops. We can cover projects from the First Crusade to the thirteenth century. The Lords of the Orient is part of the Living History Lovers Federation with The Somatophylakes, re-enacting Greeks and Macedonian phalanxes. We can thus gather more than forty fully equipped adults in a large camp. We take part in historical festivals, patrimonial exhibitions and run conferences on feudal society and thirteenth-century Oriental Latin states. We've been hired for television documentaries by Patrick Spica Productions, RMC Découverte (The

Secret of Monaco's Grimaldi Fortress) and ZED production – Curiosity (The Siege of Acre), for illustrations in books or magazines by the likes of Pen & Sword Books and Heimdal Édition. Our main activities include historical research, artefact fabrication, civil and military outfit building, sword-shield and lance-shield medieval fights, military group movements and formations, camp life and public shows.

Contacts:
E-mail: cyril.errera@hotmail.com
Website: https://lesseigneursdorient.wixsite.com/lesite
Facebook: https://www.facebook.com/Lesseigneursdorient/

Index